IMAGES
of America

WILLISTON

Members of the Whitney and Brownell families gathered for a picnic at the Brownell homestead on South Brownell Road in 1913. Samuel A. Brownell II is in the top row at center. Just below him is his brother Chauncey W. Brownell II, who maintained the homestead and farm until 1938. (Courtesy Bartlett Brownell.)

ON THE COVER. This was the Sanford D. Warren house in June 1904. From left to right are believed to be Sanford Warren and his wife, Amelia (Bradley) Warren, with Otis S. Clark, Sanford's cousin. The house and barn are at 607 North Williston Road. See page 67 for more details. (Courtesy Williston Historical Society archives.)

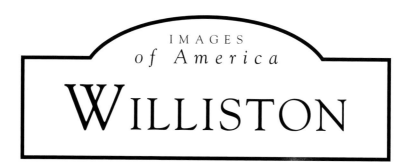

IMAGES
of America

WILLISTON

Richard H. Allen

ARCADIA
PUBLISHING

Published by Arcadia Publishing
Charleston, South Carolina

Printed in the United States of America

Library of Congress Control Number: 2021937185

For all general information, please contact Arcadia Publishing:
Telephone 843-853-2070
Fax 843-853-0044
E-mail sales@arcadiapublishing.com
For customer service and orders:
Toll-Free 1-888-313-2665

Visit us on the Internet at www.arcadiapublishing.com

To Ginger Isham, Mark Hutchins, and Brenda Perkins for their love of Williston history and support for this project.

CONTENTS

ACKNOWLEDGMENTS

Many people have helped to make this book possible by sharing their photographs, memories, and knowledge. They all deserve a well-earned thank-you for their generosity and belief in the value of saving and presenting some aspects of Williston's history.

The Williston Historical Society board of directors supported the project from day one: Brenda Perkins (president), Stephen Perkins, Adriene Katz, Meghan Cope, Terry Macaig, Cameron Clark, Peter Callas, Stacey McKenna, and Jon Stokes. Past officers and members of the Williston Historical Society deserve credit for preserving the town's history and images that form the basis of this volume.

My family—daughters Elizabeth and Jill Allen and my wife, Lucille—helped with the editing and writing. Steve Perkins, executive director of the Vermont Historical Society, aided with the editing of the introduction.

Arcadia editor Caroline Vickerson was quick to respond to questions and offered support in many aspects of the process.

Jane Kearns and Debbie Roderer, along with the staff of the Dorothy Alling Memorial Library, were extremely helpful with my requests for access to the historical society archives during the pandemic. Sarah Mason, the town clerk, was welcoming and accommodating during research in the town records.

For their help in locating appropriate images, the staff at the University of Vermont Silver Special Collections, Prudence Doherty and Chris Burns, as well as Paul Carnahan and Marjorie Strong at the Vermont Historical Society, were most helpful.

A special thank-you to Nancy Stone, Devin Colman, Jim and Lucy McCullough, Willy LaCasse, Albert LaCasse, Sandy (Carpenter) MacNair, Cameron Clark, Kay Painter, Libby (Tuthill) Roberts, Robert Bradish, Seth Urie, Jim Heltz, Bartlett Brownell, Laura Keeton, Greta Powers, Karen Shastany, and Jeneva Burroughs.

Assistance from neighboring historical societies came from Eva Clough, Jerry Fox, and Tim Jerman of the Essex Community Historical Society; Karen Yaggy in Richmond; and Jean Miner in Hinesburg.

The many people and organizations who gave permission to use their photographs are noted in the captions. I am grateful for their participation and support. Images from the Williston Historical Society archives are noted with WHS in the courtesy lines.

INTRODUCTION

The town now called Williston is part of Ndakinna, the ancestral home of the Abenaki since the retreat of the last glaciers almost 12,000 years ago. Paleoindians left traces of their seasonal settlement at what is known as the Mahan site near Allen Brook. The 5,000 stone artifacts unearthed there give insight into the local activities and extensive trade networks of these early inhabitants. For example, most of the stone artifacts are made from local quartzite and chert, but the remains of other tools are made from stone from as far away as modern-day Maine and Pennsylvania. Other sites in the area illustrate how the Abenaki and their ancestors adapted to the changing climate, developing technology such as pottery, various projectile points, and agricultural systems. Nearly 100 archeological sites around town attest to thousands of years of human occupation.

For the English, who established permanent settlements in southern New England in the 1600s, the area that would become Williston was a new frontier. As the population in Massachusetts and Connecticut grew, southern New Englanders eyed the New Hampshire Grants, as Vermont was then known, with interest. In 1763, the governor of New Hampshire, Benning Wentworth, issued a charter to 65 men for the town of Williston. As absentee land speculators, it is likely none of them set foot in the town.

Settlement of the 23,000-acre Williston charter began in 1773 when Thomas Chittenden and Jonathan Spafford explored the area. They bought land along the Winooski River and built cabins to solidify their land claims. By the summer of 1774, there were about 40 settlers in town.

Thomas Chittenden, who went on to become Vermont's first governor, has always been a point of pride for Williston. His grand brick home burned in 1926, but his son Giles's home still stands on Governor Chittenden Road. The Truman Chittenden house on Route 2 east of Williston Village also remains. The Chittenden family's accomplishments have been frequently commemorated over the years, from a monument to Thomas in 1896 to a statue in 1998.

Those who moved to Williston in its early years did so for the fertile land in the Winooski River Valley and the towering forests. They must have viewed Williston with much the same perspective as the 1882 *Gazetteer and Business Directory of Chittenden County*, which described Williston as "admirably adapted to agriculture; it contains some hills but is mostly a fine level country, undulating in some parts, with just enough hollow and dale to lend a pleasing diversity."

Settlers established subsistence farms that yielded most of what they needed as well as sawmills on Allen Brook and Muddy Brook to take advantage of the abundant timber. Larger water-powered industries clustered around Hubbel's Falls on the Essex side of the Winooski River.

As the population increased, the infrastructure developed to enhance transportation and trade. Chartered in 1805, the Winooski Turnpike covered the 36 miles from the Burlington courthouse, through Williston, to Montpelier (modern US Route 2). Its prominence in Williston's early days may be seen in the many 19th-century property records that give the turnpike as a reference point when describing the boundaries of a farm or lot.

The turnpike proved essential to Williston's early economy. Several inns were established along the way, including Eagle Hall, located in the northeast quadrant of the four corners of the village from 1827 to 1856.

Conflicts in the nation's first century echoed locally in Williston. The story is told that during the War of 1812, sick soldiers garrisoned in Burlington's Battery Park were sent to a "pest house" in Williston for quarantine. Remains of these men were discovered behind Muddy Brook School. Superintendent of schools Jackson Miller, unable to locate surviving descendants, reinterred the remains. Prompted by a letter Williston native John A. Forbes wrote to the local chapter of the National Society United States Daughters of 1812, the organization honored these men with a monument dedicated in 1933 in the Eldridge Cemetery in South Burlington.

Vermonters moved away from subsistence farming in the 1820s to raise sheep. When the economic factors discouraged the production of wool, the newly thriving railroads supported an expansion of dairy farming, with butter and cheese production and eventually the shipment of milk to markets. The impact of the railroad was most evident in North Williston starting in 1849. The area soon had a school, post office, general store, depot, and several industries.

Throughout the 19th century, the residents of Williston established schools. The first public schools were simple, wood-heated structures where a single teacher taught all students from grades one to eight. One-room schools were sited around the town to serve the students nearby. Several of these structures have survived as residences; the Stovepipe Corner School, moved from its initial location to the town green and restored, is a quintessential example.

The schools also provided employment for many locals. Besides teachers, residents were paid to transport students, to saw and pile wood to heat the schoolhouses, and to perform upkeep on the buildings themselves. Some school supplies came from the local stores of Roswell E. Brown and Kenneth Aseltine. The town boosted its own economy through the town budget.

The Williston Academy was established in 1828 and lent a contrast to the one-room schoolhouses. In 1861, Williston Academy's curriculum included common English, higher English, Latin, Greek, and music, which was the most expensive course at $10 per term. The academy gained a reputation for excellence during Joseph Cilley's principalship (1858–1868). The 1866 school pamphlet praised Williston, declaring the town "free from haunts of idleness and dissipation" and "favorable to good order, to mental improvement, and moral culture." When the academy closed around 1883, the building became part of the town school system.

Williston's spiritual and social life was centered around the churches erected in the village: the Congregational Church in 1832, the first Methodist in 1842, the Universalist in 1860, and the second Methodist (Federated) in 1869.

The Civil War (1861–1865) pulled many able-bodied men away from home. All told, nearly 130 men from Williston served to defeat the Confederacy.

Some returned safely, while others were not so fortunate. Rev. Joseph Sargent, pastor of the Universalist Church, signed up volunteers, served as chaplain of the Vermont 13th Infantry, contracted typhoid, and died in Virginia. Charles B. Chapin, who served in the 1st Vermont Cavalry, survived capture and the horrors of Andersonville Prison only to die two months after his release from malnutrition.

One Civil War veteran offers a glimpse into the lives of Vermont's small black population. Newell Cyrus Langley, an African American born in Hinesburg, served in the Massachusetts 54th Infantry and saw action at the Battle of Olustee in Florida. After the war, he moved to Williston to farm with his wife, Harriet, and his father. He died in 1892 and is buried in the Morse Cemetery on Route 2A.

Insights into Williston life in the late 19th century come from Dr. Albert L. Bingham, who practiced medicine in town from 1875 to 1917. He reflected on his work and the town to Dr. John B. Wheeler, as written in *Memoirs of a Small-Town Surgeon*:

> Many country doctors talk as if they had the hardest lives in the world, but I don't find it so. Any way of getting a living has its disagreeable side, and long drives, broken sleep

and irregular meals are the doctor's discomforts. They trouble some people a good deal, but really, I don't mind them much. I'd a lot rather have them than the annoyances that lawyers, teachers, or businessmen have to put up with. And then Williston isn't by any means a bad place to live in. It's a well-to-do-town and I guess, figuring on the proportion of expenses to income, that I couldn't make a much better living anywhere than I do here. There's a nice, friendly lot of people here. They seem to appreciate what I try to do for them. Don't believe I have an enemy in the whole place and many of the people are mighty good friends. Then there's another thing. There's no lawyer in Williston. Now I don't know anything about law, but I do know a good deal about these people that I've lived among all my life, and if I do say it, I think I have a knack for smoothing out differences among folks. Result is, they have a good deal of confidence in me. . . . They come to me with a good many little misunderstandings and quarrels that they would take to a lawyer if one was handy. I can generally manage to patch things up and I know I have staved off a quite a number of lawsuits.

Still another thing. There's no Catholic Church in Williston. There are a good many Catholics here, but they go to church in Burlington or Essex Junction. And they've got so they come to me with lots of the little things that they would take to the priest if he wasn't so far away—private family matters, whether I thought young So-and-So was the right kind of fellow for Mary to be going with, whether Jimmy had better be sent to college or kept on the farm, what to do about Dan, who is getting to drink too much, and so on. Some of the Protestants come to me in the same way, too, though they've got a good minister of their own. . . . I've come to be a kind of little Pope in Williston, and I like it. Makes me feel like I am really accomplishing something, even if it is in a pretty small corner.

In the century following the Civil War, the population of Williston often declined, hitting a low of 929 people in 1920. At that time, the town featured numerous dairy farms, a picturesque village along Route 2 with a few stores, a small economic hub in North Williston, many dirt roads, and a small-town culture. Throughout the early part of the 20th century, the Federated Church dominated the scene, as did organizations like the Grange, Good Will Club, 4-H, Boy Scouts, and Camp Fire Girls. Also, the Chittenden Camp (No. 12,415) of the Modern Woodmen of America was chartered on November 26, 1906, as the local chapter of this national fraternal benefit society.

The Universalist Hall (the present town hall) and the Modern Woodmen of America Hall (the present town hall annex) served as community gathering places for dances, suppers, card parties, minstrel shows, speakers, and other entertainment.

Local resident Ruth Painter's interviews, buttressed with statistics, vividly depicted life in Williston during the 1920s. Both horses and cars traveled the roads, so there was a need for what the Lunderville brothers offered at the Brick Store, which was converted into a garage that sold Socony gasoline and Firestone tires. They advertised a blacksmith shop in back. Private bus service and the railroad also provided transportation. Because electricity was still missing from most homes, radios were powered with batteries, and ice was cut for refrigeration.

Williston's sense of peaceful remove was shattered in the 1927 flood. The Winooski River escaped its banks, damaging North Williston and the farms below French Hill. The town's road expenses increased significantly from 1927 to 1928, with much of that devoted to repairing the ravages of the flood.

The Great Depression and pre–World War II years fostered much debate about the poor condition of roads, both at the state and town level. Dirt roads, constructed for horse-drawn vehicles, proved inadequate for the faster ones powered by internal combustion engines. "Hard road" advocates wanted a statewide effort to promote paving, but meager state budgets often put a check on this.

Meanwhile, the primitive Williston roads did have an upside. Many people realized extra income through the upkeep of roads and bridges, snow removal, erecting snow fences, delivering gravel, and cutting brush. A close reading of past town reports shows that the public was, in fact, the town's public works department.

A perspective on Williston during the Great Depression comes from newspapers and town reports. In 1932, Sheriff Paul Dimick noticed an increase in chicken stealing in Essex and Williston that he did not believe "was the organized work of outlaws" but rather "thieves working independently." The overseer of the poor detailed requests for help with groceries, rent, firewood, clothing, and medicine. In 1933, overseer Clarence Caswell spent $159 "assisting 264 tramps."

In 1934, the town took advantage of federal money from the Civil Works Administration to employ 70 men and 13 teams to work on road projects. In addition, voters were given a choice to keep the town budget down by considering whether to fund the opening of winter roads and raising money for the illumination of streetlights. They voted no on both options.

During World War II, Williston did its part in providing men and women for the armed forces. The 1946 town report lists over 100 names on the honor roll of those who served, five from the LaCasse family alone.

On the home front, the town had a Civil Defense Committee and raised funds for the Red Cross, war stamps and bonds, and the United Service Organizations. Scrap drives involved everyone, including schoolchildren. The money raised was divided among local groups such as King's Daughters, the Grange, and the Nursing Association.

Williston was proud of its observation post located south of the Johnson farm where the northbound lane of Interstate 89 is today. Established on April 12, 1942, to keep track of planes in the Burlington area, the post was staffed 24 hours a day by residents and people from surrounding towns. The *Burlington Free Press* reported diverse spotters: the entire select board, a clergyman, the postmistress, three schoolteachers, active and retired farmers, numerous "housewives," an orchestra leader, waitresses, and others. The town report noted that 150 people had volunteered their time.

During the postwar years, the population increased in Williston and the rest of Chittenden County. A burgeoning economy, the baby boom, and the opening of IBM in Essex changed the face of Williston. The town turned from its agricultural roots to more of a suburban bedroom community. Farmland was transformed for housing developments, especially along Route 2A. Williston Central School, built after the Village School burned in 1949, became the continually expanding nexus of a newly flourishing educational system. The town's concerns now included zoning and planning, water and sewage, recreation, a consolidated high school district, police, and a fire department.

The trend toward suburbanization continued in the early 1960s when the interstate highway split the town in half. Some farms were devastated; at the same time, the commute from Williston to both Burlington and Montpelier was made easier. Commercial construction began around Taft Corners, the interstate area, and later Marshall Avenue.

Besides this shopping district, today the historic Williston Village has the town offices, the library, Brick Church, Central School, and Recreation Path. In between, neighborhoods offer housing options from apartments and condominiums to single-family homes. South of the interstate, several farms, Mud Pond, Lake Iroquois, and Brownell Mountain give testament to the open land from Williston's more rural past. North of the interstate, the Catamount Community Forest and Williston Golf Course provide recreational opportunities. A few working dairy farms remain along the Winooski River.

The Williston of today may be summed up in its motto "Old town charm, new town spirit."

One

THE VILLAGE AND BEYOND

In the past, the four corners area of the village has seen two general stores, a blacksmith shop, a creamery, two schools, an inn, a bandstand, the town library, and the post office in three locations. Today, the Federated Church has taken the place of Eagle Hall, one store remains, and the post office has moved out of the village. There is an access point for the Recreation Path and such stately structures as the Solomon Miller Greek Revival house, the Warren house with a Federal-inspired presentation, and a Gothic Revival home that add to the attractiveness of this area.

In addition, the village has been the home of the government buildings that provide services to the citizens. The town hall has moved on numerous occasions from one building to another. The library has also seen different homes until settled in its current location in 1959. The fire station has similarly moved three times before locating to the west on Route 2.

The establishment of the armory in 1958 by the state government added a new dimension to the cluster of brick buildings in the village center. The siting of the Village School and the Central School added to the importance to this center of town.

Churches have also complemented the village streetscape. The tall white spire on the Federated Church is an area landmark. The Brick Church (1832) has become a town-owned building and now hosts a variety of activities. The Immaculate Heart of Mary Church was constructed later, just on the outskirts of the village. Two original churches have been repurposed several times over and now serve as the town hall and the town hall annex.

Some other successful businesses were located outside the village, such as Twist O'Hill Lodge, the Oak Hill Creamery, and Maple View Farm and Cabins.

Based primarily on the Federal and Greek Revival architecture, the Williston Village Historic District was established in 1979 and expanded in 1992. Except for the 1958 demolition of the 1842 town hall, Williston deserves credit for protecting these historic buildings in the village and retaining its appeal.

In 1827, Benjamin Going announced in an ad in the *Sentinel and Democrat* newspaper that Eagle Hall, a "commodious house," was open for business on the northeast section of the four corners in the village. It was "fitted up with extensive dining and promenade rooms, and pleasant drawing and lodging rooms." It served the community in a wide variety of capacities until it burned down in 1856. Besides providing room and board for travelers, it was the site of political conventions, legal proceedings, auctions, meetings, social events, and a medical office. This recent artwork by Charles Newsham depicts the way it might have looked in 1845. (Courtesy WHS.)

In 1885, Charles D. Warren purchased this store from Henry Joslyn. It stood directly opposite the Federated Church on the south side of Williston Road. The store was also the post office, and a symbol for telephone service was displayed beside the front door. It was the frequent target of burglars around the turn of the 20th century. In 1901, one break-in set off an alarm and a Wild West–style shootout that resulted in escaped culprits and no injuries. (Courtesy WHS.)

This is another view of the Warren store, with the Solomon Miller house in the background. As was the tradition in Williston and other Vermont towns, the postmaster was often a store owner. Charles Warren's daughter Sylvia was the postmistress here from 1914 to 1951. She was also the town librarian, hired in 1905 when she was 19. In 1929, the book collection was moved from the Modern Woodmen of America's hall to the second floor of the store, making Sylvia's two jobs a bit easier. (Courtesy WHS.)

This house, occupied by Judge William Miller, was on the east side of Oak Hill Road just south of the four corners in the village where there are an impressive number of black locust trees. According to the family history, the house was burned down in September 1877 by a man who was sent to prison by Miller. Several items were saved from the fire, including a primitive oil portrait of Elisha Miller Sr. and his second wife, Sarah. The painting is now part of the Williston Historical Society collection. (Courtesy WHS.)

This is a 1908 view of the 1840 Solomon Miller house with its Greek Revival architecture. It was the home of two Williston doctors: Alvin C. Welch and Albert L. Bingham. The house passed from the Bingham family to Jack and Betty Bradish in 1939. Their son Robert remembers the high ceilings, sliding down the curved stairway bannister, a busy house where his parents ran a restaurant and later the post office and rental units, watching thunderstorms from the cupola, and decorating the tree on the corner with Christmas lights. (Courtesy WHS.)

Dr. Albert L. Bingham completed medical studies at the University of Vermont (UVM) in 1875 and started his practice in Williston soon thereafter. He was active in his field through the county and state medical societies. He served in the legislature as a representative and as a senator. He lived in the Solomon Miller house with his first wife, Jennie Welch, daughter of Abigail and Dr. Alvin C. Welch. Jennie died in 1906, and Bingham married Julia McLaughlin of Peacham in 1908. According to Dr. John B. Wheeler, "He was a country doctor who thoroughly enjoyed his work and . . . was very successful in it." (Courtesy Shirley Miles and Ginger Isham.)

The pre-1800 Talcott/Warren House at 8210 Williston Road is where David Talcott Jr. operated a tannery using the water from Allen Brook. The back portion predates the grand presentation of the Federal style in front and its now generous porch. This 1896 image shows the extended Warren family. From left to right are (first row) Sylvia, unidentified boy, Mildred, and unidentified girl; (second row) Josie (Patterson) Warren, Kate (Patterson) Ames, Mary (Cutter) Patterson, James Patterson, and Charles Warren. The house was purchased by Howard and Terry Carpenter in 1964. (Courtesy Cameron Clark.)

This c. 1898 photograph of the Warren family shows, from left to right, Sylvia, Charles, Mildred, and Josie in back. Josephine Patterson of Shelburne and Charles Warren were married in 1886. Charles taught in country schools before he purchased a store. He was described as having a "cordial disposition, [and] excellent judgment in business matters." He was the town clerk and town treasurer, and served in the state legislature and as a school director. All except Mildred acted as the Williston postmaster/mistress during most of the years they ran the store. (Courtesy Cameron Clark.)

This image, probably from the 1950s, shows the Kenneth Aseltine store in the village at the four corners, operated by "the ultimate gentleman" from 1924 to 1963 as an IGA affiliate. The c. 1913 building had a hardware section where one could get glass cut for a window and buy nails, screws, and paint. Aseltine had a large water-filled cooler in front of the counter for cold drinks and would help some children buy penny candy. Shirley Miles remembers if her children got too rambunctious inside the store, he would pick them up and sit them on the counter. According to Jim McCullough, the store "specialized in Mr. Aseltine. It also carried most menu essentials, as long as they were eggs, bacon, milk, canned goods, snacks, and candy. He also stocked a size run of black rubber boots and Red Ball sneakers. His was the quintessential Vermont general store, minus the Round Oak parlor stove." It is now the Korner Kwik Stop owned by Bernard Perreault since 1987. (Courtesy Special Collections, UVM.)

The Federated Church was built from 1867 to 1869 and dedicated on October 6, 1869. It superseded the 1842 Methodist church (now the town hall annex) and became a federated congregation when the Congregationalists (Brick Church) agreed to join them in 1899. In this photograph, the four corners and Federated Church are seen around 1938. (Courtesy WHS.)

A 1907 report by George F. Wells called this "the leading federated church in Vermont. . . . The spirit of worship has been enriched by better preaching, larger congregations, and a new fellowship. . . . Williston is a typical average New England town in which the best in the Puritan tone of life is remarkably persistent. The French Catholic population is increasing rapidly. In every respect the federation is declared to be a success. . . . It is a decided step in advance in the solution of the religious problem of one country town." (The 1907 bandstand pictured here was moved in 1927 to the golf course grounds.) (Courtesy WHS.)

The Junior Choir Festival at the Federated Church was started in 1959 by music director Terry Carpenter, Gertrude Urie, and Cathy Yandell. Choirs were invited from neighboring churches. The festival gave the children the motivation to practice and perform in front of a large audience. The popularity and success of the festival has led to its continuation to this day. It has been renamed the Terry Carpenter Junior Choir Festival. This photograph was taken around 1963. (Courtesy Sandy [Carpenter] MacNair.)

These Junior Choir members of the Federated Church around 1961 are, from left to right, (first row) Marcia Urie, Marion Isham, Jackie Mercia, and Hope Yandell; (second row) Mary Merchant, Margaret Isham, and Laurel Swift. (Courtesy Sandy [Carpenter] MacNair.)

On February 1, 1833, the *Burlington Free Press* noted that the Brick Church "is well suited to its use and is highly . . . credible to the society. . . . It is sufficiently large to accommodate six or eight hundred people. In the plan and execution, it combines convenience with simple elegance and good taste. The interior is in modern style. The pulpit is very low; the seats are slips; and there is only one gallery . . . for the choir. In all respects the edifice is such that 'the blue-eyed goddess' of architecture may look down upon it, if not with pride, at least complacency." (Courtesy WHS.)

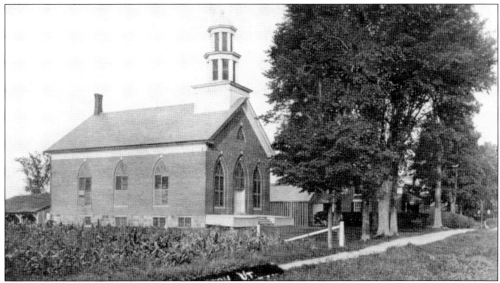

The 1832 Brick Church, a blend of Greek Revival and Gothic Revival styles, was built for the Congregationalists. It was their home until 1899, when they joined with the Methodists to create the Federated Church. The carriage sheds are visible out back, and the snow porch in front allowed people to board their carriages and sleighs without stepping into the cold and wet slush on the ground. The building, owned by the town and available to rent, is home of the Brick Church Music Series, which sponsors a variety of artists and provides fundraising opportunities for local nonprofits. (Courtesy WHS.)

This was the Federated Church Methodist Youth Fellowship that took on the 1963–1965 cleaning and restoration of the Brick Church. Windowpanes were replaced, debris taken away, some of the original furniture located, and donations were collected to further the effort. Mark Hutchins (third row, far left with glasses) was the main instigator of the undertaking. He received a national award of merit from the American Association for State and Local History, the youngest person ever to receive it. The list of young people and adults grew as the project gained notice and support. (Courtesy WHS.)

This 1953 image shows the Immaculate Heart of Mary buildings with the rectory (constructed around 1875) on the left and the first church that was constructed from the remodeled barn and carriage house. The cinder block wall erected to provide privacy for the Carmelite nuns is evident around the house. On June 3, 1951, the first public Mass was held in the church. A shrine dedicated to Our Lady of Mount Carmel was built on the property in 1954. The nuns left for Barre in 1968, having stayed in Williston for 18 years. (Courtesy Immaculate Heart of Mary Church.)

A 1984 history of the Immaculate Heart of Mary Church reported serious deficiencies in the 1951 building: weakened trusses, heat loss, and a cold, damp cellar. Given the state of the building and a growing parish population, the construction of a new church took on increased urgency. Ground was broken in 1991 for the present church, and the first public Mass took place in April 1992. This image shows the two churches standing side by side for a short time after the present church, right, was built and before the 1951 church was torn down. (Courtesy Immaculate Heart of Mary Church.)

Sylvia Warren was Williston's first librarian, from 1905 to 1955. Here, she is seated on the steps of the Warren store where the library was located from 1929 to 1959. (Courtesy WHS.)

The Dorothy Alling Memorial Library opened in December 1959 and was dedicated the following April. Frank Alling, who donated the library in memory of his wife, and David Yandell, chairman of the board of trustees, spoke at the ceremony. Librarian Betty Hart said, "It's a beautiful place. I have a polished mahogany desk and . . . a needlepoint chair." Volunteer Jeneva "Pat" Peterson remembered the first card catalog as a pull-out drawer, minimal hours, and a lack of knowledge on the part of the helpers. There was now space to hold up to 5,000 books and a basement for storage and book binding. (Courtesy Dorothy Alling Memorial Library.)

Betty Hart was hired as the librarian in 1956 at $3 a week to supervise the library in the Warren store building. It was open only during the warmer months. Before Williston Central School established its own library, the town library served the schoolchildren and teachers. Here, Hart helps some children sign out books in 1961. She served until 1969, when Adelaide Lane was appointed librarian. (Courtesy WHS.)

Rickie Emerson (center) served as the director of the Dorothy Alling Memorial Library from 1976 to September 18, 2005. She oversaw the two additions to the library in 1986 and 1998. Joining her in this 2005 photograph are Susan Blair, youth services assistant (left), and Debbie Roderer, assistant director. (Courtesy Dorothy Alling Memorial Library.)

From left to right, a Miss Northrop, Margaretta Page, Rex the dog, and Arthur E. Page pose in front of the Universalist parsonage on August 19, 1896, the day of the Thomas Chittenden Monument dedication in the Chittenden Cemetery. Built around 1838, this house was the second U̶⸻⸻list Church parsonage, from 1884 to 1906. The present address is 7970 Williston Road, t̶ longtime Williston educators Carter Smith and Joy Peterson and the Williston Vill̶ is just west of the Lyon's apartment building. (Courtesy WHS.)

This Italianate-style house, built in 1839 at 7997 Williston Road, has a long history connected with the Brick Store across the street, as it was owned by store owners and workers. Later, the house provided Dr. John C. Lantman and his family suitable living space and enough area for his medical practice on the east (right) side. It is now the home of the Ridgeline Real Estate Company. (Courtesy WHS.)

On June 12, 1994, a dedication ceremony for a bench on the Recreation Path was held to honor Dr. John C. Lantman for his years of service to the community. He opened his practice in 1954 and retired in 1993. Former patients remember a very caring physician who made house calls, kept his stethoscope inside his shirt to keep it warm, and had a ready supply of lollipops for the children. Pictured here are, from left to right, Dr. Louis Wainer, Lantman's mentor from Hinesburg; Dr. Lantman; and Lantman's wife, Claire Lantman. (Courtesy Kimberly [Lantman] Parker.)

This was the streetscape in the heart of the village in the early 1900s. From left to right, the Universalist Church (1860), with its tall steeple removed, had become the Universalist Hall in 1913 (now the town hall); the Methodist church (1842) was purchased by the Modern Woodmen of America and housed the library and a meeting space for the King's Daughters (now the town hall annex). The old town hall (1842) was torn down in 1958 after serving as the first home for the Williston Fire Department; and the Village School (Williston Academy, 1869) burned in 1949. (Courtesy WHS.)

In 1958, some changes were underway with the brick buildings in the center of the village. On the left, the volunteer firemen were putting an addition on Chittenden Memorial Town Hall (1842 Methodist church) to house the fire department. At right is the 1842 town hall, which had been the home of the fire department. It was torn down to make room for the parking lot of the soon-to-be-built Vermont National Guard Armory. (Courtesy Robert Bradish and WHS.)

Before this Vermont National Guard Armory was built in 1958, the 1954 town report had printed a letter from Maj. Robert H. Ray thanking the citizens and select board for the use of the Modern Woodmen of America hall as the home of B Battery of the 206th Field Artillery Battalion from Ethan Allen Air Force Base. After construction, this building was named the Major General Francis W. Billado Armory in honor of the adjutant general of the Vermont National Guard who was instrumental in promoting the construction of nine armories around the state. (Courtesy Town of Williston.)

The 1961 post office was constructed by postmaster Jack Bradish, rural carrier Robert Alberts, and substitute carrier Haultsay Shortsleeves and was leased to the postal service. It was next to the exit for Williston Central School. After serving several other functions, including as fire department headquarters during the construction of the 2006 fire station, it was torn down in 2007. With increased population and business in town, the post office was transferred to a building on Commerce Street off Route 2 west of Taft Corners and later to Blair Park. (Courtesy WHS.)

In 1939, Postmaster General James A. Farley traveled to Vermont for the annual meeting of the New England Postmasters' Association. Given his role as chair of the Democratic National Committee, a top advisor to Pres. Franklin D. Roosevelt, and speculation that he was interested in pursuing the presidential nomination in 1940, he was given the royal treatment of an escorted caravan, luncheon in Montpelier, and visits to a number of post offices along the way to Burlington. His 4:10 p.m. stop on June 27 in Williston was proceeded by Richmond, Jonesville, Bolton, Waterbury, and Middlesex. The public was invited "to greet and shake hands" with Farley. The visit created this photographic opportunity for Farley and the town. The three people front and center are, from left to right, 90-year-old former Burlington mayor James Edmund Burke, Williston postmistress Sylvia Warren, and Farley. Burke, born in Williston in 1849, was influential in arranging Farley's visit to Vermont. (Courtesy WHS.)

The 1842 town hall was modified to accommodate the fire department formed in 1949 by Howard Lunderville and Roland Osborne. The siren on top of the building and a phone network notified the 12 volunteers of fires. A 1931 American LaFrance fire engine was available to handle the five calls in the first year. Lunderville said the very first call was a gas tank that blew up, sailed 30 feet in the air, and destroyed the chicken coop it landed on. Funds were raised for the department through auctions, food sales, a minstrel show, and charging $50 after each call. (Courtesy WHS.)

Seventeen members of the recently established Williston Fire Department pose with their badges affixed to their coats in January 1953. From left to right are (first row) William Lane, Robert Alberts, Haultsay Shortsleeves, Roy Lunderville, Adrian Fortier, Lynwood Osborne, Lester Lunderville, Stuart Talcott, Oskar Stapel, Ernest Gaudette, Edward Roberts, Chief Howard Lunderville, and Assistant Chief Roland Osborne; (second row) Paul Dufresne, Emerson Miles Jr., Preston Charland, and Paul Roberts. (Courtesy Gertrude Gonyo, WHS.)

Starting their 20th year, the 1968 fire department answered 45 calls, including fires in the Brownell Mountain forest, at the S.T. Griswold horse barn, and at the Marvin Clark barn. A new International 1,000-gallon pumper, at the cost of $20,000, was now on hand. The town was praised for the installation of a water system that allowed a fire hydrant every 500 feet. The department was now supported in part by $4,000 from the town budget. (Courtesy Joyce Goodrich.)

In October 1988, presidential candidate George H.W. Bush (center) visited Williston for a campaign rally in the fire station. Here, he poses with some members of the fire department. Bush gave Chief Howard Lunderville a Dalmatian puppy, and he lamented that now he had to find someone to take care of it. Bush won in Vermont with 51 percent of the vote; in Williston, he garnered 53 percent. (Courtesy Joyce Goodrich.)

Here, the Brick Store (c. 1894) has the name of the operator painted over, but it is marked as the post office. Over the course of its life, it suffered two devastating fires, in 1851 and 1902. In 1920, it sold tires, Hood's tennis wear, Louden's barn fixtures, and Pine Tree milkers. In the 1950s, the store had farm and dairy supplies: Kow-Kare, Bag Balm, louse powders, feed, Diversol, bar brooms, and salt. It also sold television sets and bottled gas. Today, it is the Lyon's apartment building at 7986 Williston Road. (Courtesy WHS.)

George Pease owned the Brick Store for 34 years. He bought it from Smith Wright for $2,100 in 1884 and sold it to John Forville in 1918. The store advertised dry goods, groceries, boots, shoes, drugs, medicines, paper hangings, farm tools, clothing, hats, and caps. Pease was an out-of-town landlord; he lived in Burlington, where in 1905 he started the Essex Manufacturing Company, which produced white duck clothing for steamship employees and the Pullman Company. He married Williston resident Julia A. Clark in 1883, and they lived with her parents, Jason and Juliana Clark, for a time. (Courtesy WHS.)

Carl and Gertrude Urie bought Romeo Houle's store in 1968 and operated it until 1977. Their son Seth recalled the creemee sales with two popular flavors—maple and black raspberry. One year he convinced his parents to advertise opening day, and the resulting lines were so long, they interfered with the rest of the business. "Mom and Dad swore they would never advertise again. . . . Gas and ice cream were not big moneymakers, but they got people to stop, and many would buy something else. I got an education in retail sales watching and listening to my parents run Urie's Market." (Courtesy Seth Urie.)

Jack and Betty Bradish opened the Old Brick House Inn and Tea Room in their home (the Solomon Miller house) in February 1940 and operated it until April 1941. A menu from July 30, 1940, offered a full-course, fried chicken meal from appetizer to dessert for $1. After returning from the war, Jack attended the Fanny Farmer Cooking School in Boston on the GI Bill. This business card was for the Carriage House restaurant, which ran from November 1946 to November 1949. Emerson Miles Jr. remembers the restaurant was famous for its onion soup. (Courtesy WHS.)

SURE LUCK CABINS – U.S. ROUTE 2 – WILLISTON, VERMONT

The Sure Luck Cabins were east of the Thomas Chittenden Cemetery at 8397 Williston Road. In the 1955–1956 *Vermont Visitors' Handbook*, the proprietors were listed as Mr. and Mrs. J.A. Nault. It offered a "quiet, comfortable farmhouse, [with] double and single cabins, excellent beds, toilets, hot and cold water . . . [and] reasonable rates." (Courtesy WHS.)

This July 5, 1948, real estate photograph is labeled "remodeled old house," which indicates what was the "Belle A. Johnson showcase" would soon become the Elmcrest Inn. The inn was open year-round, served three meals a day (dinners from $1.50), and specialized in teas, club meetings, bridge parties, and receptions. Due to the lack of a reliable water supply, within a year it was sold. It was eventually turned into a cloistered monastery for the Carmelite nuns in 1950 and is now part of the Immaculate Heart of Mary parish west of the village. (Courtesy WHS.)

Some businesses were located beyond the village. Twist O' Hill Lodge opened on June 10, 1931, with Marjorie Luce of Waterbury as the proprietor. The new structure on French Hill hosted weddings, meetings, and special occasions. There were large porches on two sides and a main dining room with a hardwood floor for dancing. The view of the Winooski River Valley and the Green Mountains was a major attraction. Eight rooms upstairs and two cabins accommodated overnight guests. Within a year, a house across the road and an additional nine acres was purchased to expand the lodgings. (Courtesy WHS.)

Twist O' Hill Lodge, as advertised in 1935, was on a "fine cement road," close to a golf course, and nine miles from Burlington. Other attractions "within driving distance" included "Smugglers' Notch, the Islands, [and] Lake Willoughby." It was "[w]here modern equipment and management unite with old time charm to make the visitor welcome to Vermont's beautiful scenery." The season ran from May 15 to October 30. (Courtesy WHS.)

Maple View Farm and Cabins, with Blossom F. Goodrich as proprietor, was on Route 2 next to the Richmond town line. The log cabins had screened porches, showers, and cooking privileges. Rooms were also available in the house. In 1955, the rates were $2 to $2.50 a day, and the season ran from May 1 to November 1. The house is at 10236 Williston Road, the home of Paquette Full of Posies Nursery. (Courtesy Special Collections, UVM.)

Herbert and Rita Goodrich started the Pine Crest campground in 1967 on their property south of Route 2, west of the village. The campground was open from Memorial Day to the end of November, and the original cost for a campsite was $3 a day. Over the years, the amenities included a pond stocked with fish, an in-ground pool, and utility hookups. Most of the maintenance, cleaning, and bookkeeping was taken care of by Rita. After closure in 1988, it became the Pinecrest Village neighborhood on Timothy Way. (Courtesy WHS.)

The Oak Hill Creamery was in the part of town known as Talcott, near the intersection of Old Creamery and Oak Hill Roads. A post office (1897–1903), a schoolhouse (1858–1950), and a blacksmith shop served the area. Hiram Walston built the creamery in 1868; Lewis H. Talcott managed it for many years. David Isham Talcott took over ownership in 1895. Art Senna remembered "a great long building with an apartment house on one end and a little store in the middle." One summer, Ken Bessette Sr. had a job working on a farm on South Road, and part of his responsibility was to take the milk from the farm to the creamery each morning. He traveled across the road south of Mud Pond. He recalled buying penny candy in a very dark, small store attached to the creamery. The pigs kept in back from spring to fall were fed with the leftovers from the cheese and butter operation. The Burlington newspapers recognized Talcott as a locale by giving it its own news column in its heyday. Below is a 1920 advertisement for the store. The creamery is pictured above around 1905. (Both, courtesy WHS.)

Wilbur C. Sawyer took this photograph of the Samuel A. Brownell II sawmill from the Williston side of the Winooski River around 1899. The mill produced boards, beams, firewood, shingles, lath, and clapboards. Brownell was born in Williston in 1842. He settled in Essex Junction, built the Brownell Block, and financed the Brownell Library. A Christmas tradition at the homestead in Williston was to take gift cigars off the tree, each with a message, and pass them out. Brownell did not smoke and was kidded by his brother Chauncey W. Brownell II with the following poem: "Down by the river under the hill / There stands, they say, a big saw mill; / Now on the left as you go down / Or on the right as you're coming to town, / Sam built for himself since autumn came / A wonderful structure, 'office' by name. / He fitted it up most wondrously fine / With chairs and tables all made of pine, / And a bargain stove from a railroad car / To make all complete needs this one cigar." The office appears at center in this image, just to the right of the covered bridge. (Courtesy Vermont Historical Society.)

Two

NORTH WILLISTON

In many ways, North Williston was a separate community within the town. With a school, store, post office, telephone exchange, railroad depot, creamery, and various industries, it had many aspects of an almost self-sufficient village. It prospered with the arrival of the railroad and declined when the trains no longer stopped there, a pattern that was repeated throughout the state.

The rich soil of the Winooski River Valley supported some successful farms here. The Chapmans, the Fontaines, the Doenges, and the Fay family have all contributed to this agricultural history. The Whitcomb family's North Williston Cattle Company has operated here since 1992, maintaining the farming tradition.

Most buildings from the heyday of North Williston are gone, but the schoolhouse has remained as a residence, along with several other houses dating from the 19th century. Three bridges have spanned the river since 1860 to connect North Williston to communities to the north, and today, North Williston Road has become an important and busy commuter route in the county. Chapman Lane to the east and Fay Lane to the west allow travelers a view of the quieter side of Williston.

Much of what is known and appreciated of the unique nature of this community over 100 years ago is due to the remembrances of Julia (Mentzer) Fifield. She recalled "North Williston at its best" upon moving there in 1918. The Mentzers quickly established themselves in the community. Her father, Charles, worked for the Smith Wright Company and won a seat on the select board. He took on various agricultural projects and advocated for road improvements throughout the state. Julia and her friend Julia Wright became accomplished equestrians and young explorers of what the area had to offer. She also left a rich oral and photographic history of North Williston, some of which is shared in this chapter and in the 2011 publication *North Williston: Down Depot Hill.*

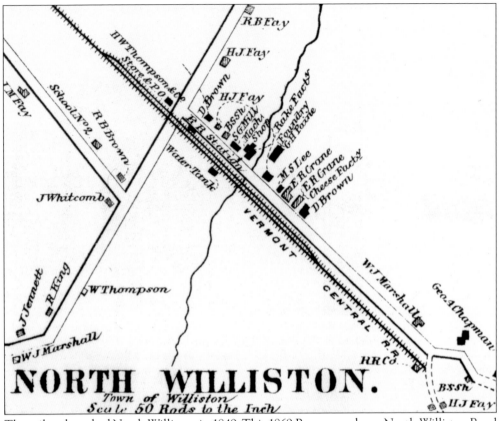

NORTH WILLISTON.
Town of Williston
Scale 50 Rods to the Inch

The railroad reached North Williston in 1849. This 1869 Beers map shows North Williston Road from top to bottom. Fay Lane branches off to the left, and Chapman Lane runs parallel to the railroad tracks. The businesses along Chapman Lane were a blacksmith, gristmill, machine shop, rake factory, foundry, and cheese factory. H.W. Thompson operated the store and post office. Note the predominance of the Fay family in the area. (Public domain.)

North Williston was an economic engine for the area with the Smith Wright cold storage plant, Brown's butter tub factory, a creamery, the depot, and a covered bridge across the river. This photograph of North Williston was taken from Bean Hill in the early 1900s. The school is on the far left, the two brick homesteads at the entrance to Fay Lane are front and center, and in the distance at right are the industries on Chapman Lane. (Courtesy WHS.)

In this view looking east is the depot in North Williston around 1910. It was south of the tracks close to North Williston Road. It was built in 1867 and had a waiting room, freight rooms, and an office for the agent. Julia (Mentzer) Fifield lived nearby in the early 1900s and loved to spend time in the depot learning about the telegraph. Even though she preferred riding her horse to school in Essex Junction, she often took the train in rainy weather. (Courtesy WHS.)

The Smith Wright cold storage plant was a unique and important business in the area from around 1871 to 1934, when this building in North Williston burned down. The company specialized in products that could be kept on ice cut from Chapman's Cove and then shipped out on the rails. The slaughtering and packing of poultry provided seasonal employment for locals. After Wright died in 1899, his sons Clinton, Clayton, and Homer carried on the business. (Courtesy Julia [Mentzer] Fifield.)

A railroad section crew on a hand-pump cart was a common sight in North Williston in the early 1900s. They would inspect the tracks, replace rails and ties as needed, and do general maintenance. After the 1927 flood, there were an estimated 300 workers in North Williston repairing the damage to the tracks and other rail infrastructure. The railbed was totally rebuilt from Williston to North Duxbury. (Courtesy Gertrude Gonyo.)

The note on the back of this postcard says that this crew, led by a Mr. Simmons (white shirt), installed the first electrical line into North Williston. The hydroelectric plant at Hubbel's Falls, the largest in the state at the time, came online in May 1917 and was probably the source of the North Williston electricity. In October 1918, the line extended up North Williston Road to Frank Talcott's farm, where lights were installed. For Blossom Goodrich, below French Hill, the power for his farm came from Richmond. Telephone service had arrived in town in 1897. (Courtesy WHS.)

Wilbur C. Sawyer took this photograph at river level of the North Williston double-lane covered bridge across the Winooski River around 1900. The bridge was built in 1860 with intricate stonework to create the abutments. The cost was shared by Essex, Underhill, Jericho, and Williston. The bridge allowed farmers and other residents in nearby parts of Essex and Jericho direct access to the rail line, the creamery, and the store. (Courtesy Vermont Historical Society.)

After 63 years of withstanding the elements, the North Williston covered bridge was taken out by ice on April 7, 1923. It headed downstream and threatened the railroad trestle but eventually broke apart. Part of it ended up on property of the Redmond farm, and the lumber was recycled into a building. The other section of the bridge lodged against the dam at Hubbel's Falls and was dismantled. The replacement bridge seemed equally jinxed. In February 1925, while still under construction, the structure was also swept away by high water and ice. (Courtesy WHS.)

The Chapman family farmed in North Williston from the early 1840s and continued for five generations. The farm took advantage of the rich bottomland but was also prone to flooding, such as in 1927. At right is Chapman's Cove, the source of ice for the cold storage plant and area homes. In the background is Saxon Hill in the town of Essex. (Courtesy Connie [Chapman] Dumas.)

Walter E. Doenges and his wife, Ada, celebrated their 40th wedding anniversary in 1967 at their home in North Williston with over 100 family members and friends. The list of community organizations that were benefited by the couple is long: 4-H group, Home Demonstration, Federated Church, and the cancer fund drive. Walter was active in the County Farm Bureau, the Grange, and Young Farmers Group. He served as president of the Chittenden County Farm Bureau and was a farm labor agent for the state. He also served on the town select board and in the state legislature from 1958 to 1961. (Courtesy WHS.)

Julia (Mentzer) Fifield lived in North Williston from 1918 to 1923 in the house at 2588 North Williston Road. Her fond memories included exploring the countryside, visiting the depot and the store, dances in the Universalist Hall, horseback riding on Dolly with pal Julia Wright, and ice cutting on Chapman's Cove. "The years in North Williston were so perfect that it is almost impossible for me to translate it all into writings. For me life was enchanting. I was a fanciful child and a happy child," she wrote. (Courtesy Julia [Mentzer] Fifield.)

The Roswell E. Brown store in North Williston was "a community gathering place," according to Marvin "Bob" Chapman. It was especially busy after the farmers delivered their milk to the creamery and then gathered to trade news and gossip. The store also held the post office and telephone exchange. A wide variety of items were available, from clothes, groceries, tools, and hardware to farm implements and feed for animals. The common practice was to charge the merchandise and deal with a bill at the end of the month. (Courtesy Gertrude Gonyo.)

Julia Martin and Roswell E. Brown were married on September 4, 1879. She was born in Corunna, Michigan, and was a charter member of the King's Daughters in Williston. They had three sons, Arthur, Albert Carlisle, and Charles. Roswell's father, Reed Brown, had a butter tub factory in North Williston that Roswell was involved with for about 10 years. He ran the general store in North Williston from 1894 to around 1933. He also represented Williston in the legislature in 1898. Julia (Mentzer) Fifield said he was "a sprightly man, small in stature, soft spoken, and very much a businessman." He was patient with his customers, "especially children." (Both, courtesy of Jim and Lucy McCullough.)

McCORMICK-DEERING
FARM MACHINES
R. E. BROWN
NORTH WILLISTON, VT.

Since Roswell E. Brown was a dealer of McCormick-Deering farm implements, he was cited in an announcement for the celebration of the centenary anniversary of the invention of the McCormick reaper. The field day was held April 18, 1931, in the Modern Woodmen of America Hall (now the town hall annex). It included a five-reel motion picture, *Romance of the Reaper*, "a graphic description of the progress made by the reaper since the first reaper was made 100 years ago. Progress in the development of harvest machinery is climaxed with the showing of a fleet of harvester-threshers harvesting 640 acres a day. A reproduction of the first reaper will be exhibited." About three hundred 1831 reaper reproductions were built to accommodate the schedule of the celebration across the country. It was a major publicity campaign for the International Harvester Company and included free meals, publications, and over one million commemorative medals passed out as souvenirs. Williston was chosen for this event probably because of its central location, its farming community, and the availability of the hall. This sign was posted at the Brown store. (Courtesy WHS.)

Roswell Bishop Fay and Ann Cutler married in 1833. In 1838, they moved to North Williston from Richmond and raised five children. Fay engaged in farming and lumber manufacturing and represented the town in the state legislature. Their residence was where the Fontaine house now stands, just before the bridge on the east side of North Williston Road. Ann died in 1870, and in 1886, Roswell moved to California, where his daughter Cynthia and son Alfred lived. He died there at age 97 and was buried in the East Cemetery in Williston. (Both, courtesy of Jim and Lucy McCullough.)

Three

FAMILIES AND FARMS

Williston has a history of family farms, as evidenced by the images in this chapter. Looking back over the 20th century, one can get a sense of the triumphs and tragedies of this way of life.

In 1901, Lewis H. Talcott found himself out 118 cattle and $2,000 when many of his herd tested positive for bovine tuberculosis. The state cattle commission oversaw the process, and he was "compensated fairly" for the animals, but the slaughter was very controversial and gave town folks something to talk about before and after the event, according to the *Burlington Free Press*.

Bad luck hit John Pratt, who lost his farm and house to fire in 1926, only to lose them all again when the Winooski River flooded in 1927. Unlike structures, family cannot be replaced, and Pratt did carry his mother to safety.

Thriving farms were highlighted in the *Burlington Free Press* during the Depression. Frank and Laura Metcalf bought 117 acres of land near Taft Corners. They started out living in tents for the first six months during the construction of their home. As they increased their dairy herd, Laura's teaching income helped retire their debt. In 1930, they were deemed triumphant due to hard work and "stick-to-itiveness." The LaCasse family was featured in a 1939 article with their ability to pay off the farm and raise 12 children. Their achievements were gained with "lots of ambition" and "a capacity for hard work."

Farming was celebrated with a forestry field day on the Talcott farm in 1949, and two years later, the Chittenden County Farm-Home days were held in North Williston at the Walter Doenges farm. Interspersed among the accomplishments of farming was the constant threat of barn fires that hit many over the years.

In 1953, poultry farmer Al Pillsbury was elected overseer of the Thomas Chittenden Grange. His farm made the news again in 1955 because a White Leghorn hen laid a "monster" egg of "just about perfect . . . shape" weighing "two and a half times heavier" than an average egg. The only downside, noted by the Chittenden County agricultural agent, was "Wow, that must have hurt."

Today, Williston farms supply maple products, apples, vegetables, berries, beef, pork, Christmas trees, and hemp. The Whitcomb's North Williston Cattle Company, the Clark farm (Riverhill Farms Inc.), and the historic Johnson farm continue with a dairy focus. Windswept Farm, Imajica, and Riverhill Farms are equestrian centers. To be successful, farmers in Vermont diversify and adapt to changing markets and technology.

The Brennan family pose in front of their Jericho farmhouse around 1903. From left to right are Paul holding a chicken; Arthur with a cat; their mother, Mary Jane; and their father, James. This was the family that established the Brennan line in Williston on Mountain View Road in 1915. James and Mary Jane were the children of Irish immigrants. (Courtesy Margaret [Roy] Portelance.)

James and Mary Jane Brennan are pictured at their farm on Mountain View Road between 1915 and 1923. Her 1918 diary entries tell of family activities: tapping trees and boiling sap, plowing with a colt, sawing wood at Muddy Brook, selling 250 pounds of maple sugar in Essex for 20¢ a pound, and selling beans and potatoes in "the city." (Courtesy Margaret [Roy] Portelance.)

This c. 1916 photograph shows the Brownell house with a Cadillac pickup truck parked close to the front porch. The house was built in 1829 by Jotham Hall and sold to Chauncey Wells Brownell I in 1841. It became the focal point of the Brownell homestead. It was purchased by John Heins in 1942. The present address is 3188 South Brownell Road, the home of the Imajica Equestrian Center. (Courtesy Bartlett Brownell.)

This was part of the haying process at the Brownell homestead cow barn around 1934. Chauncey Wells Brownell II is front and center with his hat and pitchfork. His grandson Lincoln C. Brownell stands in the back of the truck. Reflecting the juncture of power on the farm, the loose hay was brought in by horse-drawn wagon and tractors. Note the woman in front with the essential bucket and dipper to refresh the crew. (Courtesy Bartlett Brownell.)

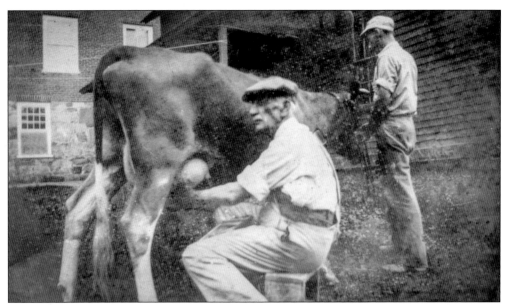

Chauncey Wells Brownell II, a UVM and Albany Law School graduate, was on the board of several companies and utilities in Burlington. He also served in the legislature and was Vermont secretary of state for eight years. His professional income kept the Brownell farm going with a farm manager and paid staff. "Outside of his professional life, he was the most quiet, thoughtful, gentle, generous person I have almost ever known," wrote his grandson Lincoln C. Brownell. This c. 1930 photograph shows Chauncey milking a cow behind the homestead. (Courtesy Bartlett Brownell.)

The centennial of the Brownell house was celebrated in September 1929 with a family reunion at the homestead and included this multigenerational dance on the lawn. A dinner for about 40 people was hosted by Chauncey Wells Brownell II and his daughter E. Mabel Brownell. The family history was recounted, along with some farm milestones involving Morgan horses, Merino sheep, and Ayrshire cattle. (Courtesy Bartlett Brownell.)

This was the original Thomas and Elizabeth Chittenden brick home erected on Governor Chittenden Road around 1787. There was a ballroom on the third floor and a fireplace in each room. In June 1926, when occupied by Wright Clark and family, the house was destroyed by fire. Newspaper descriptions lamented the irreplaceable antiques lost and the unique inverted-Y structure of the huge chimneys designed to accommodate the numerous fireplaces in the historic mansion. Two spindle back chairs used by Thomas and Elizabeth were saved. (Courtesy Cameron Clark.)

The Clark farm was established on the Chittenden property in 1835 by Wright Clark and his father, Paul. Later named Riverhill Farms Inc., the farm has continued in the family for eight generations, now operated by Patrice Maloney and her daughter Cameron Clark. This was one of the original barns on the farm, built sometime in the mid-1800s. It was used for housing and milking up to 60 dairy cows and 60 youngstock as well as herd bulls and work horses. The 286-foot-long barn was destroyed by fire in June 1968. (Courtesy Cameron Clark.)

According to his 1917 draft registration, Wright Clark was a corporal in the military unit at Michigan Agricultural College (Michigan State) for two years. In November 1917, he went to Boston to take the exam for the Aviation Corps. He trained in Princeton, New Jersey; Americus, Georgia; and at Ellington Field in Texas. In the summer of 1919, Lieutenant Clark was discharged at Camp Devens in Massachusetts. In August, the town welcomed the soldiers home with a celebration where Clark, Walker Degree, and Horatio Curtis described Army life; the Richmond band provided music. (Courtesy Cameron Clark.)

During August 1956, 1957, 1959, and 1960, the New York Football Giants held training camp at St. Michael's College. Warm days, cool nights, and little rain were prime attractions for the team. The scrimmages were exceedingly popular, with up to 3,000 fans attending. This 1959 image shows, from left to right, fullback Phil King, Williston host farmer Marvin Clark, and place kicker Pat Summerall posing for a publicity shot to promote Farm Tours, which were part of the Champlain Festival, a celebration of the 350th anniversary of Samuel de Champlain's exploration of the lake in 1609. (Courtesy Cameron Clark.)

Hiram and Charlotte Murray were married in Canada in 1843. It was his second marriage. They established a prosperous farm (now owned by the Ishams) on Oak Hill Road that was detailed in Hiram's will after his death in 1864. The value of the furniture, kitchenware, farm implements, animals, crops, buildings, and land shows that Hiram had provided well for his family. The farm was passed on to their daughter Laura and her husband, Truman Naramore, after their 1865 marriage. The Naramores sold the farm in 1871 to Jarius Isham for $10,000 with a sugar orchard, apple orchard, and three barns. Laura and Truman owned a considerable amount of real estate in town before their departure for California. (Both, courtesy of Jim and Lucy McCullough.)

After barely surviving the horrors of Andersonville Prison during the Civil War, Truman Crossman Naramore married Laura Murray. They settled in town for 19 years, and he turned to farming and patenting farm implements, such as a rock and stump lifter manufactured by the St. Albans Foundry. The family moved to California in 1884, where he continued with his inventions, including a hay press, and delved into real estate during the Los Angeles boom. Naramore continually sought an increase in his Civil War pension and was active in the local chapter of the Grand Army of the Republic. The warmer climate eased his war-related symptoms, but a property venture led to his murder in 1895. (Both, courtesy of Jim and Lucy McCullough.)

Mary (Comstock) Isham and her husband, Jairus, front row at right, appear with other family members in this late-1800s photograph. This couple established the Isham farm on Oak Hill Road in 1871, where they raised their family. The farm was transferred to their son Homer, who carried on the Isham farming tradition that is still going strong. The former dairy farm with a Jersey herd has transformed with greater diversification including Christmas trees, berries, maple sugaring, an events barn, and a farmer's market, all under the guidance of Michael Isham and Helen Weston, the fifth generation to work the land. (Courtesy Ginger Isham.)

This image of the Hiram and Charlotte Murray house appeared on the 1857 Walling map of Chittenden County. The Gothic Revival style was popular in the mid-19th century, here characterized by the steeply pitched roof and detailed wooden trim. Today, this Isham house looks remarkably like it did in the 1800s, although it contains several apartments and has undergone some modern updates. (Courtesy Special Collections, UVM.)

Ginger and David Isham (left) were married on October 17, 1959, in the Bristol Federated Church. They met at a dance at Jacques' Barn in Huntington when Ginger was 16 years old. She worked at the Mount Philo Inn for several summers to cover the $110 tuition at the Fanny Allen Practical Nursing School for one year. David had worked on the farm continually, and since his brothers had other jobs, he was the son who purchased it in 1973 from his parents, Sylvia and George Isham, who appear at right. (Courtesy Ginger Isham.)

Pictured are George and Sylvia Isham in 1983. Ginger Isham remembers George as an avid fan of *Reader's Digest*. Sylvia was noted for her crazy quilts and the prodigious canning of vegetables to feed 13 children, who all had farm chores. Family fun came with lawn games, swimming in Lake Iroquois in the summer, and sliding and skating in the winter. The couple were members of the Good Will Club that was formed in 1921 to provide "showers and parties on happy occasions, and aid to the needy and a helping hand in sorrow," according to the *Burlington Free Press*. (Courtesy Ginger Isham.)

This September 1905 image shows the Walker farm on South Brownell Road that was owned by Lewis H. Talcott. Note the favorite things that the family members proudly pose with—a dog on the porch, a horse, a bicycle, and a team hitched to a wagon full of milk cans. The farm was purchased by Oliver and Nora LaCasse in 1925. (Courtesy WHS.)

Oliver "Pete" LaCasse was born in Farnham, Quebec, in 1887. His son Albert said, "He was stern in a happy way. He was very interested in what we all did. . . . None of us had a lot of education. We didn't like school, and he needed the help at home. . . . He knew farming. . . . [Both parents] were both very good with their money. They were good businesspeople. They would pay us. We would get enough to buy our clothes and go out on Saturday night." (Courtesy Willy LaCasse.)

Nora Blain was born in Quebec in 1888. She moved to Burlington and worked as a seamstress at Abernathy's clothing store. She married Oliver LaCasse in 1910, and they raised 12 children. Son Albert remembered his mother: "She would have a flower garden, a fish pool with running water . . . in the milk house. . . . She had a vegetable garden, which we all pitched in on. . . . Every spare minute she had, if she had any, she raised chickens and sold eggs." (Courtesy Willy LaCasse.)

This was the LaCasse family at their house on South Brownell Road around 1930. From left to right are (first row) Albert, Clarence, Billy in father Oliver's lap, mother Nora, Lena, Marion, and Raymond; (second row) Frankie, Madeline, Helen, Margarite "Tootsie" in front of Helen, Lucille, and Catherine. When the 260-acre farm was purchased in 1925, it included two bay horses, 34 Jersey cows, and some farm equipment. In 1939, they hoped to pay off the farm that had 100 pigs, over 50 head of cattle, two horses, and all the modern conveniences. William and Dorothy LaCasse continued farming here until 1985. (Courtesy WHS.)

Pvt. Albert LaCasse entered the service in 1943 and served in an antiaircraft unit in North Africa. In 1941, he started a successful boxing career in Vermont. Out of 40 professional fights, he won or drew 38. Sports writers described him as "clever and tough," a "speedster," and "scrappy" when he was rated as "Vermont's lightweight king" in 1946. He and his brother Raymond trained and fought in Memorial Auditorium in Burlington as well as across the state. Albert's fighting name was taken from his brother's pronouncing his name as "Bub"; in the family, he was "Bubby." When he started fighting, they changed it to "Bobby." (Courtesy WHS.)

This is an early-1900s view of the Giles Chittenden house on Governor Chittenden Road. Smith Wright purchased the farm in 1873, and it has been in the family to this day. It is the home of Jim and Lucy McCullough, who established the Catamount Outdoor Family Center there. Since 2019, the nearly 400 acres of surrounding land make up the Catamount Community Forest, protected from development and open to the public for recreation. (Courtesy WHS.)

This c. 1946 photograph shows the Wright/McCullough house from the south and the Holstein cows that replaced the Jersey herd. On the left is Frank Lashua; he and his wife, Clara, worked for the family for 42 years. A Mr. Sinclair, longtime farm foreman, is at center, and the third man at right is unidentified. The small house on the right was the Smith Wright and Sons office building that stood in North Williston. It was moved to this location after the 1934 fire destroyed the main cold storage buildings of the company by the railroad tracks. (Courtesy Jim and Lucy McCullough.)

This 1945 photograph at the Wright farm shows Mary Fay McCullough mounted on her donkey Eee-haw with her father, James D. McCullough, at her side. Son Jim described his father as a "stereotypical southern gentleman to the core in all matters." The building with the peaked roof was the icehouse of Smith Wright's cold storage operation, where processed poultry was stored before it was transferred to the plant along the tracks in North Williston. (Courtesy Jim and Lucy McCullough.)

In April 1967, Jim McCullough wanted to get to his job site so he could get home in time to complete his income tax form. But he was hampered by a non-functioning Jeep and a motorcycle that quit. So he turned to his gelding Pawnee and rode four and a half miles to work in Richmond and back. The *Burlington Free Press* entitled this photograph, "Uncle Sam Blues." McCullough has been a Williston representative in the state legislature since 2003. (Courtesy Jim and Lucy McCullough.)

In this c. 1908 photograph taken at the Wright farm of a Stevens-Duryea automobile, Clayton Wright and Anna (Talcott) Gawn are seated in front. In the backseat, Cynthia Talcott (left) is holding Julia Wright (later McCullough), and Abbie Fay Wright is embracing Janet Gawn. Standing in back are Walter Gawn (left) and George Talcott. Clayton and his twin Clinton were noted as the local dealers for the Stevens-Duryea Company in a 1909 newspaper advertisement. They were later listed as automobile merchants from 1915 to 1924 in *Walton's Vermont Register*. (Courtesy WHS.)

Elisha Miller Jr. was brought to Williston by his parents from Wallingford, Vermont, in an oxcart in midwinter when he was one and a half years old. Angeline (Munson) Miller, as a 21-year-old, remembered when General Lafayette passed through Williston in 1825; he stood up in his carriage drawn by several pairs of white horses, took off his cocked hat, and bowed to the crowd. Angeline was remembered as an artist and gardener. She and Elisha were married in 1826. In 1850, they moved part of their original house and many of the outbuildings from the banks of Muddy Brook uphill to establish Maplehill as the family homestead. The prosperous farm included a sawmill on the brook. (Both, courtesy WHS.)

This was the Miller homestead, affectionately known as Maplehill. The dairy farm had market gardens (note the greenhouse) and a great number of outbuildings. The 300-acre farm was passed down to their son Jackson, then to his daughter Laura Miller Parker. In 1987, the Williston Historical Society tried to save the house, but it was soon torn down, and the land was developed along the intersection of Industrial Avenue and Williston Road. (Courtesy WHS.)

Jackson Miller served the town as a teacher, school director, superintendent of schools, justice of the peace, and selectman. Along with his brother Norman, he was a market gardener at the Miller homestead, taking their produce to Burlington to sell. In the fall, he would take trips to the Adirondacks for camping and hunting. One obituary described him as a "great lover of nature and true sportsman." (Courtesy WHS.)

Laura Miller sat for this photograph on her 75th birthday in 1868 and was all dressed up for the occasion. Her brother Elisha Miller Jr. asked to be based in Vermont as a soldier during the War of 1812 because he feared for her safety. Although courted when she was a young teacher, she never wed. Instead, she dwelt with her brother William. As the oldest girl in a family with 14 children, she mothered her younger siblings at home, then helped raise William's three children. At her death, she was the longest-standing member of the Congregationalist Church, having joined more than 60 years before. (Courtesy WHS.)

Lewis H. Talcott was photographed on March 29, 1897. He was born in Williston, the son of Roswell and Lodisa (Holt) Talcott. He married Lucy Root in 1858, the daughter of Zimri Root and sister of Henry Root. Lewis and Lucy had five children. During the Civil War, he went to California and engaged in dairying. He returned to Williston, expanded his farmland and dairying operations, and became very prosperous. (Courtesy WHS.)

This c. 1900 photograph of the Fay/Talcott Farm (1860) with the large, still-standing barns on North Williston Road is indicative of the agricultural reach of Lewis H. Talcott. At their peak, his farms totaled about 2,000 acres and 300 cows, which supplied milk to produce butter and cheese at the Oak Hill Creamery, making him one of the most successful farmers in the state. For many years he was the manager of the creamery that was built on the original farm established by his great-grandfather Deacon David Talcott. (Courtesy WHS.)

This was the Caswell family around 1875. From left to right are Susan, Flora, Clarence, and Seymour. The family came from Huntington in 1864 and built the house and farm at 943–945 North Williston Road. A Burlington newspaper reported in 1892 that "Clarence Caswell and Miss [Veretta] Clark of Underhill were married last week; so, every one in town smokes cigars now." Clarence served the town in numerous capacities, including selectman and in the state legislature. The farm passed to Clarence and Veretta, then to Howard and Annie (Caswell) Merrill, then to Carl and Gertrude (Merrill) Urie. (Courtesy Seth Urie.)

This 1903 photograph of the Caswell house and family shows, from left to right, (first row) Veretta, Susan, Annie (seven years old), and Seymour Caswell; (second row) Clarence Caswell, George Senna, David Tarbox, and an unidentified man. Evidently any bad feelings between Clarence Caswell and Albert and George Senna, when they pled guilty in 1899 to stealing grain from each other, was settled. Note the milk cans on the porch. (Courtesy Seth Urie.)

This c. 1950 photograph shows the Urie farm on North Williston Road at the intersection of Mountain View and Governor Chittenden Roads. Carl and Gertrude Urie purchased the farm in 1946 from her parents, Howard and Annie (Caswell) Merrill. The Uries had an award-winning registered Guernsey herd on their roughly 180-acre SquareWoods Farm. They sold the farm in 1965 and built a house at the end of Old Stage Road, where they eventually had 35 acres with 40,000 Christmas trees. (Courtesy Seth Urie.)

On March 1, 1959, there was a double celebration of wedding anniversaries. Carl and Gertrude Urie (left) marked their 15th, and Annie and Howard Merrill, Gertrude's parents, their 40th. Gertrude's Williston remembrances of the 1920s and 1930s included corn husking bees, card parties, skiing over fences attached to a horse-drawn sled as her mom drove up and down the road, warding off head bruises while skating by wearing a sponge under her hat, sliding down Depot Hill at night all the way to the tracks, and activities at church, the Grange, and 4-H. (Courtesy Seth Urie.)

Built around 1860, this was the Sanford D. Warren house in 1904. It is assumed that from left to right are Warren and his wife, Amelia (Bradley) Warren; Otis S. Clark, Addie Porter's father; and an unidentified woman. After Amelia's death in 1905, Sanford married Addie A. Porter in 1906. The back of this photograph is labeled, "For Abel, From S.D.W. June 8, 1904." Abel O. Porter was the son of Addie and her first husband, Albro Porter. The house has been passed down through several generations from Bradley to Warren to Porter to Coutermarsh to Shortsleeves; the present owners are George R. and Patty E. Shortsleeves. (Courtesy WHS.)

In 1966, Herbert Goodrich Jr. and his daughter Linda showed off some of the bounty of their farm on Route 2 west of the village. Herb and his wife, Rita, were married in 1954, acquired the Harte farm, and raised three daughters. Herb was active in the fire department and the town government as a selectman, as well as the Lions Club and the Immaculate Heart of Mary Church. (Courtesy Joyce Goodrich.)

When Herbert Goodrich Jr. ran for a one-year term on the select board in 1992, his campaign brochure noted his previous service on the board from 1965 to 1971, his experience as a lister and as justice of the peace, a fire department member, and a farmer and local business owner. He supported "growth in moderation . . . preserving our agricultural heritage . . . and maintaining a 'slim' and effective government." (Courtesy Joyce Goodrich.)

On May 27, 1994, the Adams family cut the ribbon for the opening of their farm market on Old Stage Road. From left to right are John Adams, Gov. Howard Dean, Scott (in back), Peggy, Stephen, and agriculture commissioner George Dunsmore. Their apple orchard started with 20 trees in 1972 and steadily grew to include 900 trees and the market that now sells a wide variety of products. With daughter Kim Antonioli and son Scott on board, there are now three generations involved in this business. (Courtesy Kim Antonioli and Peggy Adams.)

Four

PEOPLE AND ORGANIZATIONS

The citizens and organizations in Williston have created the community feel in the town. With the first national census in 1791, Williston recorded a population of 469. Much like the rest of the state, the first several decades were boom years, and that number increased to 1,185 by 1810. In the 19th century, the number grew steadily to its peak in 1850 of 1,669. It would take more than 100 years for the town to reach that level again. From 1850 to 1920, the population, with one exception, dropped each decade until it hit 929. Growth was minimal until the 1960s, when there was a 115 percent upsurge, versus a 14 percent increase in the state. The 1990s saw a 56.5 percent growth. In 2020, there were a bit over 10,000 people living in Williston. Before the 2020 pandemic, it was noted that the daytime population of the town increased dramatically with the influx of workers and shoppers. One estimate put the jump at 100 percent, creating a demand on services such as the fire and police departments.

But these numbers tell only part of the story. It was and is the residents of Williston who have made it a true community.

Historically, organizations based on the agricultural nature of the town contributed to its social life: the Grange, 4-H, and Home Demonstration. The Home Dem groups provided social support for rural women with instruction on food preparation, child rearing, and other domestic skills. The Grange was active in the late 1800s providing social, political, and economic benefits to farmers. A revival of the group occurred when the Thomas Chittenden Grange, No. 531 was formed on February 24, 1937, with 72 charter members and Charles Pillsbury as master. The group purchased the Universalist Hall for $1,000 in 1940 and sold it to the town in 1977 to become the town hall.

The Good Will Club acted as a social service agency, and the King's Daughters were a long-standing fixture in town. Today, some of these associations have been replaced, but the community importance of such groups has remained.

This chapter looks at some of the interesting people and groups that have given Williston its sense of community.

This image is of Betty and Jack Bradish around 1985. They were both Vermont natives and UVM graduates. In 1939, they purchased the Solomon Miller house on the corner of Williston and Oak Hill Roads, where they raised four sons. Jack served in the Army in World War II and later became the postmaster, succeeding Sylvia Warren. He also served on the select board and school board. Betty taught at Pine Ridge School for a while. (Courtesy Robert Bradish.)

Oscar S. Peterson Sr. was the assistant town clerk under Eugene Hanson in 1947 and took over when Hanson died in office. Peterson served with just an eighth-grade education but with a background in bookkeeping in the slate industry near Rutland and a love of numbers. He served until 1953, when Beatrice Deal became the town clerk. (Courtesy Brenda Perkins.)

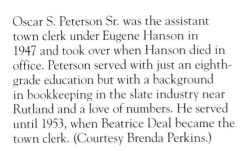

Dr. Oscar "Pete" S. Peterson Jr. and Jeneva "Pat" Peterson were married in 1936 and moved to Williston in 1944. Peterson's specialty was radiology and cancer treatment, and he held a patent for a rotational therapy unit. He served on the school board from 1951 to 1972. Pat was involved in the effort to have a centralized school built after the 1949 fire destroyed the Village School. She also volunteered at the town library for over 40 years. Here, they appear at a retirement party in 1972 after his years of service on the school board. (Courtesy Brenda Perkins.)

In 1973, the Peterson family gathered for the wedding of Brenda Peterson and Steve Perkins. Their mother, Jeneva, seated in the dress she wore at her 1936 wedding, made all the wedding gowns seen here. Standing from left to right are Brenda, Karen Boyden, Laura Keeton, Jeneva Burroughs, and Greta Powers. (Courtesy Brenda Perkins.)

This was the Peterson homestead at the end of Peterson Lane in 1954. The five girls who grew up there have some very vivid memories. Jeneva remembers: "[Our parents] purchased a small 60+ acre farm about a mile and a half out of Williston Village. We moved there in June of 1946 [with] no electricity and no running water." Laura stated: "On cold nights Daddy would heat the big iron skillet, take it upstairs to run over the sheets just before we jumped into bed, where you found your comfort spot under all the blankets and never moved all night." Karen reminisced: "[S]o many skating parties [on the pond.] Big gatherings with . . . the Urie family. Bonfires during the winter and fishing in the summer." Greta said that "horses played a big part in growing up. . . . Laurel—the tall Morgan, Rex—the circus horse, Bing, Tony, Flicker, PO-PO. Also, there are fond memories of helping to raise the whiteface calves." Brenda recalled "playing in the south pasture in an area we called Rock Village. Outcroppings of ledge and huge boulders where we had a camp, a hospital, a church and, in an old cellar hole, our house." (Courtesy Karen [Peterson] Shastany.)

Howard and Terry Carpenter were both born in small towns in 1922. Terry Coppersmith grew up in Emporium, Pennsylvania, one of nine children and one of only two to go to college. She majored in music and was a music teacher for four years in Pennsylvania. Howard's hometown was South Royalton, Vermont. They met when Howard, who was working as a mechanical engineer in the area, joined Terry's church in Emporium and sang in the choir that she accompanied. They were married and moved to Burlington in 1947. This photograph is from the early 1980s. (Courtesy Sandy [Carpenter] MacNair.)

The Carpenter family posed for this photograph at Christmas in 1959. From left to right are Cheryl, Terry holding Karen, Sandy, Howard, and David. Howard taught mechanical engineering at UVM for 40 years. He established the Williston Town Band with Herb Painter and led the project to create the bandstand. He also served as president of the historical society. Terry founded and led choirs at the church, ran the statewide Junior Choir Festival, gave piano lessons, played in a classical trio, and was an avid quilter. The love of music was shared throughout the family. (Courtesy Sandy [Carpenter] MacNair.)

This was the Painter family in 1966. From left to right are (first row) Jim, Kay, and Charlie; (second row) Herb, Ruth, Audrey, and Betsy. The family loved outdoor recreation such as skiing, hiking, biking, and tennis. Ruth and Herb had a cross-country ski shop in their barn for a time in the 1970s. Herb served on the town recreation committee and was a charter member of the Williston Ski Associates and the town band. Ruth was active in the historical society and the *Williston Whistle*, and taught at the Pine Ridge School. (Courtesy Kay Painter.)

Dorothy Lawrence Parker's formal portrait was taken on March 24, 1906, six days before her third birthday. She was the daughter of Ruel Parker and Laura Angeline (Miller) Parker. She was certainly outfitted for a Vermont winter, but playing outdoors would have been challenging. (Courtesy WHS.)

Dorothy Lawrence Parker married Francis Alling in 1932 in Winsted, Connecticut. In the 1940s and 1950s, she was instrumental in providing books for Williston children by establishing a Little Folks Library in her home with donations from local families and the state. After her death in 1958, her husband provided money to establish the Dorothy Alling Memorial Library. (Courtesy WHS.)

John Albert Forbes was a Boy Scout leader, teacher, camp counselor, and lover of history. He served on the 1913 committee that produced the town history for the 150th anniversary of its charter. He was a schoolteacher in Williston and Milton from 1911 to 1917. Inspired by his father, Frank's, service in the Civil War, he joined the 151st Depot Brigade at Camp Devens in Massachusetts during World War I. Forbes spent several years at Syracuse University and then took a position teaching at Essex Junction High School. He died at the early age of 34. (Courtesy WHS.)

Arthur E. and Margaretta Page were a fashionable couple in 1897 as they set out in their Concord buggy with steel side springs. Arthur was a merchant in the Brick Store, a traveling salesman for over 50 years for such businesses as the Standard Whip Company of Westfield, Massachusetts, and later sold fishing tackle. He was an early enthusiast at the Williston Golf Course. (Courtesy WHS.)

This 1940 photograph shows Roy Gover and his wife, Isabelle, on the Al Pillsbury farm where they worked. Roy traveled throughout Vermont with Pillsbury's McCormick combine to harvest corn and wheat. The Govers lived in several houses in town before they moved in 1934 into the renovated Sucker Hollow Schoolhouse (1875–1927) where they raised eight children. They were civilian volunteer plane spotters with the Aircraft Warning Service during World War II at the observation post in town. (Courtesy Ann [Gover] Shepard.)

First Lt. Ruth H. Mace was the daughter of Alice and Roscoe Mace. She graduated from Fanny Allen Nursing School and entered the Army Nurse Corps in 1943. She served in Michigan, Nevada, and on Guam at the Air Evacuation Hospital for six months. She was discharged on February 26, 1946. Her brother Vernon also served in the armed forces and was killed in action in the Philippines in 1942. (Courtesy WHS.)

Emile J. Boutin enlisted in early 1944 and, after flight training, joined the 8th Army Air Force as an aerial gunner on a B-24 Liberator bomber stationed in England. After six missions displaying "meritorious achievement in aerial combat," he was awarded the Air Medal. Boutin was promoted to sergeant and discharged in late 1945. He worked for Vermont Electric Cooperative in Johnson and married Betty Jane Merchant of Williston on November 27, 1947. (Courtesy WHS.)

Under the direction of Howard Carpenter and Herb Painter, this town band was formed in 1958 with 16 members. Besides playing yearly in the Fourth of July parade, in 1961 they performed at the dedication of the new post office. In 1977, the band welcomed Art and Andy Tuthill home from their 3,000-mile, cross-country bike trip. This photograph shows the group in the 1970 parade. Although not the first Williston town band, a *Burlington Free Press* article stated they were distinctive due to the "family togetherness. Quite a few fathers, mothers, and children all play different instruments and join to make this band a close-knit organization." (Courtesy WHS.)

THE

Thomas Chittenden

HEALTH CENTER

OAK HILL ROAD

WILLISTON, VERMONT

Telephone 878-8131

JOHN C. LANTMAN, M.D.   DAVID R. PARK, M.D.

WILLIAM J. RYAN, M.D.   PAUL B. STANILONIS, M.D.

"In the Practice of Family Medicine"

The Thomas Chittenden Health Center opened in 1969 on Oak Hill Road. It offered southeastern Chittenden County a family practice in a cooperative facility. It was organized by Dr. John C. Lantman and included Drs. David R. Park, William J. Ryan, and Paul B. Stanilonis. The services later expanded to include dentistry and mental health services. In 1993, the center was purchased by the Community Health Plan. (Courtesy Kimberly [Lantman] Parker.)

During World War I, the Muddy Brook Sewing Circle of the Williston Red Cross held dances to raise money. Quilts done by the circle were auctioned off, along with "the famous Isham rooster," which brought in $20, according to the *Burlington Free Press*. One dance in 1918 held at the home of Ichabod and Evelyn Isham raised $50.89. Some of the quilts were donated to the children's preventorium in Pittsford, Vermont. Muddy Brook was recognized as a distinct neighborhood in the western part of town centered around the school, Kirby Corners (Williston and Brownell Roads), and the Miller homestead. (Courtesy WHS.)

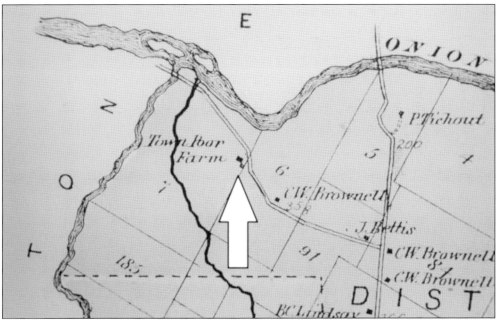

The Union Poor Farm was formed in 1859 by the towns of Shelburne, Essex, and Williston to care for indigent and needy citizens. Laura Brownell would visit the farm with her father. She later wrote that "the Poor Farm seemed like other farms, except the people did not have to work so hard. They were very meek and sometimes talked of the disgrace they had not deserved, and told the story of their lives, making [me] wonder why bad luck was always to blame." The farm, sold in 1929, was in the northwest part of town on what is now River Cove Road, as shown on this section of an 1869 Beers map. (Courtesy WHS.)

The *Williston Whistle* newspaper production team included, from left to right, (first row) Sally Bryant and Louise Ransom; (second row) Ruth Painter, Elaine Park, and Diane Goodrich. The first issue hoped "that our whistling noise will cause . . . a greater appreciation of your friends and neighbors, . . . a greater understanding of our town affairs and . . . better communicating with each other." The paper started in 1985, was sold to Paul and Marianne Apfelbaum in 1994, and became the *Williston Observer* in 2003. It was bought by Susan and Rick Cote in 2020. (Courtesy WHS.)

The Williston Women's Club was federated in the fall of 1967 for community service and social union. The club sponsored house tours and fashion shows and worked in cooperation with the Essex Community Players to raise money. The club donated to the school library, community beautification, wellness clinics, charities, and the fire department, among others. Here, the *Burlington Free Press* noted, Mrs. Robert Miller and Mrs. Joseph Carroll, cochairs of the September 1968 house tour, stand in front of the home of Mr. and Mrs. Lester Mosley. The Heins, the Stultz, and the Engisch homes were also part of the tour. (Courtesy WHS.)

Five

SCHOOLS AND CLASSES

Prior to 1950, one-room schoolhouses were located around the town to educate children in grades one through eight. They were heated by woodstoves in winter and had outhouses and later electricity. A single teacher, who boarded with a nearby family, was hired to carry on instruction for all ages. Generally, they only spent a year or two on the job, often due to low pay and the challenge of dealing with children of various abilities simultaneously.

Bartley J. Costello taught at the Muddy Brook School from 1936 to 1937. With no experience, he found the 35 students in all eight grades rather daunting. Two 14-year-old fourth-grade boys, one taller than him, were just biding their time to quit school at 16. The Christmas pageant was a big hit, bringing out parents he had never met and would never see again.

Costello boarded with the Arthur Johnson family at Taft Corners, where he had an upstairs bedroom with minimal heat and access to an unheated three-hole privy. On the weekends he hitchhiked into Burlington to stay with friends in an apartment with great food and indoor plumbing. On Saturdays, he worked all day at People's Department Store selling men's clothing for an extra $3 to add to his $18 a week teacher's pay.

With older students helping the younger ones and the hard work he put into his preparation, Costello saw results. Testing at the end of the school year demonstrated that the children of Muddy Brook School were doing well compared to the expectations for their grades. The experience made Costello appreciate the impact teachers have on their students and their future lives.

With the postwar baby boom, an increase in births prompted the citizens to consider the merits of a single school for the entire town. In 1947, the options for a consolidated school were presented by a study committee. One school in the village at a cost of $100,000 seemed "a bit excessive for a town of this size and would be difficult to finance." Other options considered had their pros and cons. One choice was to expand Muddy Brook School in a "growing part of town."

Two years later, in 1949, the Village School burned down, providing the impetus to construct Williston Central School. It expanded several times as the town's population grew, and the Allen Brook School opened in January 1997 to handle the increase in the number of students. Today, the two schools serve students from pre-kindergarten through eighth grade.

As the last one-room school that had not been renovated or torn down, the saving, moving, and rehabilitation of the Stovepipe Corner School on the corner of Mountain View Road and North Williston Road was a major undertaking for the Williston Historical Society. The 1988 move was preceded by the construction of a foundation and followed by months of carpentry, painting, and electrical and plumbing work, much with volunteer labor. Today, it stands in front of Williston Central School and is open to the public during the Fourth of July celebration and on other special occasions. (Courtesy WHS.)

Roxana Brownell, shown here in the back row, taught in the Stovepipe Corner School (District No. 12) during the 1904–1905 school year. The daughter of Agnes and Edward Brownell of Burlington, she went on to an 18-year teaching career in Burlington. This photograph was kept by Annie Caswell, standing at far left. She was the mother of Gertrude (Merrill) Urie. (Courtesy Seth Urie.)

The Lake Iroquois School was at the intersection of Oak Hill and South Roads. This 1925 photograph shows the extensive renovation underway to upgrade the building. The loose brick on the walls was a constant problem and was removed, and new windows and clapboard added. The site was improved with grading and ditching. Given the extent of the changes, the school was given the Proctor Prize of $100 to purchase equipment. When Williston Central School opened in 1950, this school closed and has been a residence since. (Courtesy WHS.)

Mary "Minnie" Donahue taught at the North Williston School from 1896 to 1898. It is difficult to imagine the challenge of dealing with such a wide range of grades, ages, and abilities. The outfits show that students knew ahead of time that photographer Wilbur C. Sawyer was coming, and that they should dress up for a class picture. The definition of "dressing up" indicates the varying degrees of wealth of the families. The shoeless children give a certain amount of poignancy to the image. Donahue, against the window shutter, was sure to wear her finest head piece for the occasion. (Courtesy Vermont Historical Society.)

This was the Muddy Brook School around 1910. It was on the north side of Route 2, halfway between Taft Corners and North Brownell Road. Constructed around 1861 for $500, the 26-by-31-foot brick building was required by deed to be "enclosed by a fence." The main entrance was through a 15-by-16-foot firewood shed. Dorothy (Parker) Alling had some misgivings about attending this school: "I always used to be ashamed of its name stuck on my district school report card. The other districts sounded so pretty and refined like Oak Hill, Lake Iroquois, and even Sucker Holler didn't sound rough." Her sister Marion (Parker) Marvin recalled how the Junior Red Cross met at the school during World War I and prepared gift boxes for American soldiers. She also remembered the day the superintendent of schools visited and passed out a toothbrush and toothpaste to each student, with accompanying instructions on appropriate dental care. The school was closed in 1950 with the opening of Williston Central School and was torn down due to the projected expense of renovation. (Courtesy WHS.)

This was the third Williston Academy building with its distinctive Italianate architectural features. It was constructed in 1869 shortly after the second building was destroyed by a suspicious fire. It was eventually turned over to the town and became the Village School in 1883. Emerson J. Miles Jr. attended school here in the late 1930s and early 1940s. He remembers Marion Higley, who taught grades one to four downstairs, and that three teachers taught grades five to eight upstairs. The bell rope had to be near a girl's desk, for the boys would pull it so hard that it would rebound into the attic, taking the trap door with it. Miles recounted the numerous tricks they played on their favorite teacher, Mildred Towers. Baby mice were placed in a box in her desk and her boots were stuffed with paper, but the time they put blocks under the rear axle of her 1938 Ford and prevented her from driving away caused the most ruckus. (Courtesy Seth Urie.)

Joseph S. Cilley's Vermont teaching career started in Underhill before he moved to Williston in 1858 to become principal of the Williston Academy. A *Vermonter* article depicted Cilley as a "strict disciplinarian, [who] insisted upon observance of the rules, and carried his oversight of his scholars beyond the school walls and the school hours. His interest in them never flagged, and his care for their mental and moral welfare was earnest and unceasing." Cilley established a solid reputation for Williston Academy as a place for a thorough education under the direction of a revered leader. (Courtesy WHS.)

The students and teacher in this c. 1895 photograph of a class in the Village School (Williston Academy building) are, from left to right, (first row) Louisa Christmas, Guy Kenyon, Wallace Chapman, Walter Bombard, Adelaide Morrill, Kate Cockle, and Amy Metcalf; (second row) Berton Kenyon, Cora Chapman, Florence Read, Lura Harbor, Ellen Read (teacher), Charles Metcalf, Alice Tilley, Jennie Burke, and Claire James. (Courtesy WHS.)

These are the younger students at the Village School in October 1898. Eva Ford taught here from 1893 to 1899. From left to right are (first row) Willie Bombard, Lena LaRochelle, Ethel LaRochelle, Hazel Bombard, Myrtle Pine, Lowell Frasher, Maggie McMahon, Flossie Bombard, unidentified, and Louis Pine; (second row) Carl Burnett, Clarence Christmas, Alice Bryant, Frank McMahon, Marjorie Bombard, Sarah Bing, Mildred Warren, and Florence Metcalf; (third row) Lucy LaRock, unidentified, George McMahon, Eva Ford (teacher), Morton Farmsworth, Jackson Miller (superintendent), Sylvia Warren, Harlie Bing, Belle Johnson, and Stella Metcalf. (Courtesy WHS.)

In the fall of 1921, the state board of education officially registered Williston High School as a two-year institution for freshmen and sophomores. It thrived throughout the 1920s and 1930s with drama presentations, field trips, and commencements. A special town meeting in June 1938 unanimously voted to discontinue the high school. After that, students wishing to go beyond eighth grade had to enroll in nearby towns, such as Essex Junction and Burlington. In this 1937 photograph, kept by Gertrude (Merrill) Urie (second row, second from right), the 18 high school students appear with their teacher, Edward Presby. (Courtesy Seth Urie.)

This view of Williston Central School shows how it looked from 1968 to 1990. The circular drive around the flagpole was the bus loop and the main entrance to the building. To the left is the two-story old gym/auditorium that was torn down during the construction of the 1991 wing and renovations. The original 1950 building runs north from the old gym/auditorium section. (Courtesy Williston Central School.)

Using the buildings of the former Twist O' Hill Lodge, W. Howard Delano opened Pine Ridge School in September 1968 for boys aged 14 to 20 with learning disabilities. The school had five full-time teachers and five tutors. Peak enrollment reached 115 students, with 100 teachers and staff. But the school lost money and closed in June 2009. The 14 buildings and 128 acres were sold in 2016 to NETS Institute for Church Planting and Revitalization, which trains men to establish churches in New England. This photograph is from 1988. (Courtesy WHS.)

Six

RECREATION

Williston accommodates many forms of recreation. Skiing on Brownell Mountain and in North Williston; boating, fishing, and swimming in Lake Iroquois; numerous trails for hiking; and snowmobiling have all found a home in town.

On a chilly spring day in 1924, a group of Boy Scouts under the leadership of John A. Forbes hiked from Essex Junction to Williston. They trekked to Downer Falls, played in Sucker Brook, visited the Downer family graves, and passed the "Big Rock." They expected a story because Forbes was a historian and teacher, but were any of them prepared for him to stop at the infamous Griswold House to recount a tale that would chill their blood more than the raw weather? At the house, Mary Sullivan fed the boys doughnuts and said that she had narrowly escaped Sally's gruesome fate because she was not there when the murderers arrived. Now huddling atop their destination of Lone Tree Hill, some boys must have thought how Sally Griswold stood alone in her house, like the tree on this hill, when she was killed in 1865; the only other person in the household was locked away by the murderers. Other Scouts might have wondered what the point was of having such a beautiful home as Sally's if her family wanted her dead. After a full day of hiking and wondering, they were home by 6:00 p.m.

Today, what the Scouts called Lone Tree Hill is commonly referred to as Five Tree Hill and is accessible from the west via the Sucker Brook Hollow Trail. Hikers cross the brook and pass the Big Rock on their way to the view at the top.

Some recreational opportunities in Williston have remained as they were in 1924 and others have been established since then. The Catamount Community Forest, the Williston Golf Course, the North Country Sportsmen Club, and the Recreational Path that connects with the Community Park are prime examples.

This c. 1927 image is labeled, from left to right, "Gramp, Caswell, Moore, Page, Hanson." These were several of the principals in the organization of the Williston Country Club, which met in January of that year. Gramp was Frank Talcott, and the others were Henry Caswell, Charles B. Moor, Arthur E. Page, and Eugene Hanson. The golf course was established on Talcott property, where it remains today. According to its website, "It was a simple layout with sand greens, coffee cans were used for the holes and a single set of hickory shafted golf clubs was shared between the few Golfers that would play each day." (Courtesy Williston Golf Club.)

This image shows George Talcott, left, and his son-in-law Ben Murray around 1960. Murray and his wife, Shirley, managed the Williston Golf Club for many years and oversaw the expansion to 18 holes in 1961 and the construction of the clubhouse. It has remained a family business to this day operated by Frank Talcott's great-grandsons Jeff Murray and Larry Keefe. (Courtesy Williston Golf Club.)

The North Country Sportsman's Club was established on 52 acres off Old Creamery Road in 1962. The founders were "active competitive and recreational trap and skeet shooters who wanted to have a local facility to hold practice and occasional competitions," according to Chris Boucher. Today, it provides recreational and competition shotgun target shooting events, new shooter instruction, and hunter education. It acts as "an ambassador for the safe practice of the shooting sports." Here is how the clubhouse appeared in the early 1970s. (Courtesy North Country Sportsman's Club.)

Families enjoy the sand and water of Lake Iroquois on August 25, 1974. The Lake Iroquois Recreation District, serving Hinesburg, Richmond, St. George, and Williston, now contains a beach area with a playground and snack bar, along with 150 acres of open land. The Red Cross swimming lessons given here are fondly remembered. The development of the area was made possible by a land purchase in 1991–1992 with funds from a variety of government sources. Originally known as Hinesburg Pond, the name was changed to Lake Iroquois in 1897. (Courtesy WHS.)

Lake Iroquois had an early reputation for good fishing with an 1866 bill introduced in the legislature to "preserve the fish," perhaps a response to the upcoming dam that would provide waterpower for the industries in Mechanicsville. An extremely low water level and an ensuing freeze in December 1908 allowed some locals to take axes to the ice and harvest the fish frozen to the bottom, which supplemented the "usual winter diet of salt pork and bacon," according to the *Orleans County Monitor*. The game warden stopped the practice after a few days. This 1899 photograph shows a man giving some youngsters a chance to try their luck. (Courtesy Hinesburg Historical Society.)

In 1975, the Taftway Honda Building southwest of Taft Corners was renovated as Skateland with a maple wood floor. It opened in April with roller skate rentals, sales, and a snack bar and became a popular recreational outlet. In August 1977, the wooden building was destroyed by a suspicious fire at an estimated $250,000 loss. It was rebuilt, as it appears in this 1985 image, and reopened in the spring of 1979. In 2001, it was reimagined as the Williston Indoor Amusement Center and Oasis Teen Dance Club. (Courtesy Special Collections, UVM.)

Miles Krans, following in the footsteps of his father, Marshall, led his own musical group that was popular throughout western Vermont. This 1950 photograph shows the Miles Krans Orchestra with well-known round and square dance caller Roy Gover at far right. Playing on Gover's reputation to bring in the fans, advertisements for upcoming dances often noted the orchestra and Gover as the caller. He also worked with the Chuck Wagon Riders, Pete's Merrymaker Orchestra, and Elmer Travers. (Courtesy Ann [Gover] Shepard.)

The Harte barn, seen here in 1957, was west of the Immaculate Heart of Mary Church on Route 2. It was one of the most popular spots for Saturday night dances in the 1940s and 1950s. In 1944, round and square dancing with Marsh Krans and his Orchestra cost 60¢ and included door prizes. When the farm was put up for sale in 1956, it was advertised as having "a fine dairy record plus fat income from barn dances." It was purchased by Herbert Goodrich Jr. and family. (Courtesy Joyce Goodrich.)

The 1956 advertisement from the *Burlington Free Press* at left and the c. 1970 photograph below, showing the car-powered ski tow and the warming hut on Brownell Mountain, reveals some of the skiing history here that goes back at least to 1935 when trails were cut by the UVM Outing Club. The university hoped to make it the center of its winter sports. In January 1954, Shattuck & Burnett Excavating Contractors announced they were constructing a ski area on the east side of the mountain and invited people to climb up and ski down before the tow was installed. In October 1955, Brownell Mountain Ski Slopes was incorporated, and amenities included a 1,000-foot rope tow, two slopes, a small shelter, lighted night skiing, and a ski school. Legal trouble developed in 1957 and 1958. A cooperative, Brownell Mountain Skiers, formed in 1965 and revived the area. Membership peaked at 60 families in 1970, but by 1977, the group was actively seeking new members with a heated shelter, night skiing, and a $50 fee regardless of family size. By 1979, it had dropped to 10 families. (Left, courtesy *Burlington Free Press*; below, courtesy Delmer Borah Jr.)

A skier takes off from the ski jump built in 1969 by the Williston Jaycees as part of the Nordic Ski Park on Redmond Road. Much of the work was done with donated services. It included a 22-meter and 40-meter ski jump (with a 40-foot tower), a warming shelter, parking, and an access road. The jump was redesigned by UVM jumper Petter Kongsli and used by the ski team during the 1970s. (Courtesy Town of Williston.)

UVM held the ski jumping portion of its Winter Carnival several times at the Williston facility, as shown in this 1975 image. In 1977, legal problems arose with the increase in liability insurance costs and the debate over who would pay for the coverage, among other issues. The Williston jump was closed. (Courtesy Libby [Tuthill] Roberts.)

Howard Carpenter recounted how an informal group of people skiing on Sunday afternoons on the Swift family Oak Hill property started thinking about a more involved setup. In 1960, Carpenter and Arthur Tuthill headed up the Williston Ski Associates and were soon joined by Marvin Chapman, Len Mercia, Charles Pillsbury, Marvin Clark, John Lantman, Herb Painter, and David Yandell. The Chapmans agreed to the use of their hill, shown here on their farm in North Williston. (Courtesy Libby [Tuthill] Roberts.)

This 1951 Chevrolet sedan was acquired for its engine to power the rope tow. It was first located at the top of the hill. Rope and pulleys were scavenged from other ski hills. Free lessons for elementary school students were offered on Saturday afternoons for four weeks. Later, a competitive program taught slalom, cross-country, and jumping. (Courtesy Libby [Tuthill] Roberts.)

Merton Carpenter supervised the loading of the rope tow at Chapman Hill in 1973. Besides the learn-to-ski course, a competitive Junior Ski program was added to the offerings in 1967. The program was successful for many reasons, and the number of adults volunteering their time was certainly among them. (Courtesy Kay Painter.)

A smiling Kay Painter displays the typical rope tow stance as she ascends Chapman Hill in North Williston in 1973. In 1974, the learn-to-ski program required skis with release bindings and runaway straps. Reflecting the basic nature of the ski area, participants were told there was no shelter or bathrooms. But the popularity of the free program was indicated by the limit of 120 skiers from grades two to eight. (Courtesy Kay Painter.)

Andrew Painter (left) and his grandson Charlie pose at Chapman Hill in 1973. Kay Painter wrote, "We used to joke about him constantly taking photos. He always had his camera around his neck. Now, I can appreciate it. I suppose history is documented by the Andrew Painters of the world." (Courtesy Kay Painter.)

This c. 1974 photograph shows the rig that was used to set tracks over the cross-country ski racecourse at the Tuthill residence. Preston Tuthill drove the Polaris Sno-Traveler, and his brother Andy added weight to the sled that laid down the tracks in the snow. In the background is a small ski jump the Tuthills built. It was used for the Torger Tokle League, a Nordic ski program in the 1970s, which met at their residence. (Courtesy Libby [Tuthill] Roberts.)

Libby (Tuthill) Roberts starts on the cross-country ski course behind the Tuthill residence in this c. 1973 photograph. The Onion River Nordic Club was formed around 1970 by the Arthur and Mary Tuthill family and others to provide for some local skiing and racing. The course crossed land owned by UVM, the golf course, and the McCulloughs. The popularity of the sport and the course created overuse and parking problems. In 1976, the McCulloughs, after meeting with the Tuthills, decided to create a network of trails on their property to serve the public. (Courtesy Libby [Tuthill] Roberts.)

Jim and Lucy McCullough started the Catamount Outdoor Family Center in 1978 as a cross-country ski area on their Governor Chittenden Road property. Over the years, the recreational opportunities have included snowshoeing, sliding, running, hiking, skating, and mountain biking. The nearly 400 acres are now conserved as the Catamount Community Forest, which is open to the public for recreation. The McCulloughs appear in this c. 1987 photograph. They are, from left to right, daughter Abbie, Jim, and Lucy. (Courtesy Jim and Lucy McCullough.)

In 1973, the children of Peter and Jean Battelle pose on cross-country skis behind their house on Oak Hill Road. From left to right are Torey, nine; Ann, five; and Tom, eight. After skiing at Cochran's and Bolton Valley, Ann graduated from Middlebury College and started her career in mogul competition. She was a national champion six times, a world champion, and a four-time Olympian. Ann has been inducted into the Vermont Sports Hall of Fame and the Vermont Ski and Snowboard Hall of Fame. She now lives in Steamboat Springs, Colorado, with her family, where she coaches skiing and soccer. (Courtesy Ann and Jean Battelle.)

This 1966 photograph is of Natalie Stultz on Tony at Juniper Hill Farm, the family residence on Route 2A. Along with her sister Melanie and brother Kevin, she would explore the country around their house on skis, on foot, and on horseback. The Downer place and cemetery was a favorite stop, and the top of Five Tree Hill was often the goal. Over the years, the rural character and open land of Williston has allowed residents a wide variety of recreational choices, such as hiking, snowmobiling, skiing, and horseback riding. (Courtesy Natalie Stultz and Melanie Stultz-Backus.)

Seven

CELEBRATIONS

Williston celebrations have changed over the years, but the ideas remain constant. During the 1838 Fourth of July observance at Muddy Brook, following dawn gunfire, Jahiel Munson organized the procession, and by 1:00 p.m., he had everyone in a bower on a hill. There was a speech about temperance and numerous toasts (done with guns and cheering, no liquor involved) led by Munson. By the 1830s, there were many temperance societies in America that extolled freedom from King Alcohol by comparing liquor to England's George III and the refusal to get drunk to the colonies' struggle for independence from him. Seen in this light, abstinence was patriotic. The Muddy Brook celebration closed with thanks to God.

In 1860, the Fourth of July festivities began with the cannon roar and the pealing of church bells. Again, a procession was led by the leading citizens to a bower where the Williston Cornet Band, the glee club, and the school chorus were featured in a program of music, speeches, sentiments, and nonalcoholic toasts. The crowd proceeded to the east part of the village for a "frugal repast" that was served on a 200-foot-long table to all in attendance, and then everyone marched back to the bower for more music and speeches. The impending crisis facing the nation by "sectionalists" and "fire-eaters" wanting to dissolve the Union were dismissed as "humbugs." The *Burlington Times* writer was confident that the future of the country was safe with the patriotism and love displayed by the citizens in attendance.

In the early 1950s, the Parent-Teacher Association sponsored Fourth of July activities for children. Reflecting the times, the 1953 headline promised "beauty queens" in the parade, and the 1954 speaker warned of the dangers of "Russianism." In both the 19th and 20th centuries, the Fourth of July provided the town with opportunities to display its patriotism.

Williston has also seen several commemorations over the years, with Thomas Chittenden's importance taking center stage: the dedication of the 1896 monument in the cemetery, the 1919 plaque in front of his home, and the 1998 monument on the village green. The 1913 and 1963 celebrations of the town charter were of noted success. Williston made headlines when it was the first Vermont town to formally note the sesquicentennial of the state in 1941.

Over the years, Williston has enjoyed noting its historic roots with numerous ceremonies and commemorations.

Henry Root was born in Williston in 1845 and earned his fortune in California with several patents for devices used on cable cars. He never forgot his hometown, though, and was instrumental in several civic projects. Given the modest size of the gravestone for Thomas Chittenden, Root requested a bill be introduced in the legislature to erect an appropriately large monument to the first governor. Since there was no room in the cemetery, Root purchased a nearby house and land, had the house torn down, and gave the land to the authorities to erect the monument. (Courtesy WHS.)

This monument to Thomas Chittenden was dedicated on August 19, 1896. Several thousand people traveled by train, carriage, and on foot to view the ceremony. Ex-governor John Barstow claimed, "In the constellation of wonderful men that guided the infant destinies of Vermont, Thomas Chittenden was the star of first magnitude. He was our patriarch. He was our Washington." The 1st Light Battery fired a 17-gun salute across the road, and Bessie B. Chittenden unveiled the monument. The orator of the day was ex-governor John Stewart, who spoke on Vermont history and Chittenden's life for more than an hour. (Courtesy WHS.)

In 1914, the community Christmas tree was decorated in front of the Brick Church and "lighted with torches and colored lanterns," reported the *Burlington Free Press*. As the children left the church, they sang carols around the tree, then crossed the street to the decorated Universalist Hall for gifts and music from a Victrola loaned by the Wright family. About 400 people attended and "the various committees did their work well in hearty cooperation and deserve the thanks of the people of the town." (Courtesy Seth Urie.)

ONE HUNDRED FIFTIETH
ANNIVERSARY
TOWN OF WILLISTON, VT.

Grand Historical Celebration, July 31, '13
Presenting the following Program:

9.30 to 11 A. M.   Historical Parade depicting the episodes of 150 years.

11.30 to 1.30 P. M.   Open Air Dinner beneath the lofty elms of Williston.

1.30 to 3.30 P. M.   Addresses by distinguished speakers.

3.30 to 5 P. M.   Outdoor Sports of every character.

5 to 7 P. M.   Reunion and Banquet of alumni of the late J. S Cilley's school.

7 to 8 P. M.   Concert by Sherman's Military Band.

8 to 10 P. M.   Historical Episodes, concluding with an elaborate display of fireworks.

EVERYBODY WELCOME
A GREAT DAY FOR WILLISTON

The Williston Historical Committee
July 14, 1913. If rainy postponed
until first fair day

Williston was chartered on June 7, 1763, by Gov. Benning Wentworth of New Hampshire. The residents celebrated the 150th anniversary of the town's beginning with a full schedule of activities on Thursday, July 31, 1913. Try to imagine two hours of "addresses by distinguished speakers." Fortunately, the speeches were interlaced with musical selections from Sherman's Band. The "outdoor sports" included a horse race, foot race, and a sack race, among others. The parade and evening pageant were the two grand highlights. (Courtesy WHS.)

The Gov. Thomas Chittenden family was represented in the 1913 parade by these riders on horseback. Frank Clark and Josie Fay (in front) played the role of the governor and his wife, Elizabeth. The younger Chittendens were represented by Wright and Mildred (Warren) Clark, Sylvia Warren, Florence Metcalf, Ella Johnson (in a striped skirt behind Josie Fay), and Charles Brown. (Courtesy WHS.)

The Order of King's Daughters was formed in New York City in 1886 for the "development of spiritual life and the stimulation of Christian activities," according to its website. The Union Circle of King's Daughters of Williston organized in 1891 and posed on Byron Johnson's front porch during the 1913 anniversary celebration. The group contributed to the community for many years, well into the 1960s. (Courtesy WHS.)

Parade spectators found a comfortable seat on the front porch of the Brick Store managed by Floyd D. Putnam. One of the attractions might have been the silver loving cups and the case of thermos bottles that were on display as prizes. The *Vermonter* later reported that "a large float, representing 'Vermont,' with the state seal, won the prize of a silver loving cup for the best historical feature." The *Burlington Free Press* estimated 3,000 people attended the events, tripling the Williston 1910 population of 1,000. (Courtesy WHS.)

These locals, dressed as original natives on the third float in the 1913 parade, had a role to play in the evening pageant. It was held in Belle (Johnson) Clark's amphitheater on the banks of Allen Brook, down the hill from what is now the Immaculate Heart of Mary Church. The *Vermonter* stated: "There were seven episodes, ranging . . . from 1764 to the present. . . . Governor Chittenden's first visit to Williston and rescue of a party of captives from the Indians, the signing of the charter, home scene at Governor Chittenden's . . . a Civil war scene, old-time industries and old-fashioned singing-school . . . the final episode, in which all who had taken part, appeared with 'America' in the back-ground and sang the national anthem." (Courtesy WHS.)

In February 1941, the town was credited with holding the first sesquicentennial observance of Vermont's statehood when the Thomas Chittenden Grange sponsored an evening of presentations, singing, and readings that covered town and state history. In August, a pageant written by Dorothy Alling recounted the town's history and genealogy using fashions from the past, many of them wedding dresses worn by direct descendants of the original owners. Songs and poems added to the program in the Federated Church. Wright and Mildred Clark, shown here as Thomas and Elizabeth Chittenden, played a role in the pageant. (Courtesy Cameron Clark.)

Two dedication ceremonies on September 24, 1944, paid tribute to the Williston people who served in World War I and II and to the seventh governor of Vermont, Martin Chittenden. A new headstone for his grave was donated by Governor Wills. The roll of honor location at the recently painted town hall, shown here, was marked with the laying of a wreath. The service flag at upper left had a star for each resident serving during the war. (Courtesy WHS.)

Gov. Phil Hoff spoke on the earthen stage to the east of the school on Sunday evening before the 1963 bicentennial pageant celebrating the town's charter. Episodes from the town history were presented that honored the Chittendens, the Talcotts, visits by President Monroe and General Lafayette, and the citizens who served the nation in war. There was also singing and dancing by the schoolchildren. The program was directed by Lois Graffam, and the script was written by Esther Urie and read by Rev. Kennon Moody. The cochairs for the pageant were Betty Hart and Jeneva Peterson. (Courtesy WHS.)

Postmaster Jack Bradish, sporting a beard grown for the 1963 town bicentennial celebration, poses in front of the 1961 post office. His beard was voted the longest in the not-too-serious judging. In the Sunday evening pageant, Bradish played the role of the bartender at Eagle Hall who apologized to General Lafayette for pushing him out of the way when he visited Williston in 1825. Historical note: Eagle Hall did not open until 1827. (Courtesy WHS.)

Karen Peterson and J. Ward Johnson pose in period dress for the 1963 town bicentennial celebration. Johnson, a beloved school bus driver and farmer, had his beard voted the "prettiest" in the beard-growing contest. Other activities included round and square dancing outside the armory with Bob Mario's band and Joe Chittenden as caller, a chicken barbecue in the school, historical exhibits in the town hall, and a memorial service at the Thomas Chittenden monument in the cemetery. (Courtesy WHS.)

Harold Lyon drove the convertible for Miss Vermont, Melissa Hetzel, in the 1963 town bicentennial parade. Lyon was a state prison guard, representative to the legislature, and Williston town clerk and treasurer. He and his wife, Margaret, owned the Brick Store building that became Lyon's Apartments in the center of the village. Many of the early photographs in this book were given to the Williston Historical Society by the couple. (Courtesy WHS.)

Delmer Borah Sr. played the role of Vermont's fourth governor, Isaac Tichenor, in the 1963 parade. In his report, James Brennan, the bicentennial committee chair, wrote that "Mrs. Josephine Gentes, assisted by Mrs. Elizabeth [Betty] Hart and Walter Doenges, organized an impressive parade consisting of some 40 entries supplied by town organizations and businesses—colorful historical floats, marching bands, clowns, bicycles, fire and military equipment, preceded by a mounted patrol and color guard. . . . Judges selected winners in the following categories: most historical, most original, and most humorous." (Courtesy WHS.)

In 1976, the United States celebrated its bicentennial. In the Fourth of July parade, Uncle Sam stayed strong for 200 years by drinking Geritol. The molasses on the desk and the honey and vinegar on the floor are common ingredients in switchel, an energy drink supposedly concocted for farmers doing haying in the hot sun. (Courtesy Joyce Goodrich.)

Walter and Rhoda Stultz stand in front of their home on Route 2A in historical dress for the 1976 Fourth of July parade. Walter was a professor of anatomy and histology at the UVM School of Medicine. Rhoda brought experience in interior design and interest in historic architecture to the rehabilitation of the famous Griswold house they purchased in 1959. She researched the history of the house and wrote the description that appeared in the *Look Around Essex and Williston* publication. She was a founding member of the Williston Historical Society in 1974. (Courtesy Natalie Stultz and Melanie Stultz-Backus.)

The appearance of political candidates in parades is a common sight. During the 1976 Fourth of July parade, a decorated station wagon of Gerald Ford enthusiasts tried to convince voters to support him in the upcoming election. Taking over after President Nixon resigned, Ford was running against Jimmy Carter. In Williston, Ford received 859 votes to 543 for Carter. The Williston Fourth of July parade has become a source of pride for the community. (Courtesy Joyce Goodrich.)

Eight

Getting about the Land

Williston's relatively flat topography has aided in the construction of several major transportation corridors: the Winooski Turnpike (Route 2), the Vermont Central Railroad, and Interstate Highway 89. These routes have greatly affected the town's growth.

As transportation in town improved, the transition from horses to the internal combustion engine was not without incident. In 1908, two ladies were enjoying a Saturday afternoon carriage ride near the village when two automobiles appeared from over a hill, frightened their horse, and upset the carriage. They were thrown out and injured but taken care of immediately by the motorists. In 1909, a Mr. Huntley's horse was spooked by an automobile on Johnson's Hill. The wagon was destroyed against a telegraph pole, but Huntley was uninjured. The "automobilists" did the polite thing and helped recapture the horse, which had fled about a mile away.

Until most of the roads were paved, travel could be hampered due to mud, and snow remains a challenge to this day. Travelers had a difficult year in 1926. In January, snow drifts were so bad that two Montpelier buses with passengers spent the night and most of the next day stuck west of the village. In May, "because there was apparently no bottom to the road, a half dozen cars were stalled about a mile and a half west of the village of Williston. . . . One of the cars which stayed for two and a half hours was the Montpelier bus which was finally extracted by means of hitching a block and tackle to a telephone pole. The other cars were mostly rescued by the same device," reported the *Burlington Free Press.*

Today, Williston retains some reminders of the way roads used to be, such as the middle section of Governor Chittenden Road and the trail to Mud Pond from Oak Hill Road.

Several of the images in this chapter show how the construction of the interstate highway system in the 1960s had a tremendous impact on Williston. Commercial and residential development increased, and farmland disappeared, especially near the interchange along Route 2A.

Some aspects of the landscape, such as brooks and ponds, have not created serious barriers to local travel, but rather have provided waterpower and recreational opportunities.

Currently, there are over 70 miles of roads under the charge of the town Public Works Department. About 60 miles are paved and 10 miles are gravel roads. The rural nature of Williston remains in some areas, but generally the character of the town is now suburban, and the transportation network has played a major role in this transition.

This image of Mud Pond shows Allen Brook flowing to the north (top), Oak Hill Road to the left, and South Road on the right. As early as 1858, the preservation of the fish in the pond was discussed in the state legislature. The unique ecosystem was recognized in 1897 when a paper on "The Flora of Mud Pond" was read by Webster Lockwood and C.E. Bryant of Williston before the meeting of the Vermont Botanical Club at UVM. Today, the Mud Pond Conservation Area is 141 acres administered by the town, a home to rare plants and animals. Before the arrival of electricity in the area, it was an important source of ice for nearby farmers who had to keep their milk chilled. Local lore includes stories of cattle trapped in the mud, an impossible-to-reach bottom, and the close call by two boys who, while fishing, pulled a large eel into their boat and tried to kill it with their heavy stone anchor, which crashed through the bottom, hindering their escape back to shore. (Courtesy Orthoimagery Finder, State of Vermont.)

Muddy Brook flows out of Shelburne Pond and heads north to form the Williston-South Burlington boundary. The Miller family of Maplehill took advantage of the brook on the west side of their property, with the best fishing and swimming spots noted. This photograph from the family album shows the "Swift Hole" of Muddy Brook. There was a mill from the earliest days for sawing their lumber and carding cloth. In 1931, Boy Scout Troop No. 64 was granted use of a portion of the Miller property along the brook for a campsite with plans to build a cabin, trails, and roads. (Courtesy WHS.)

Sucker Brook and its many tributaries drain southwestern Williston and St. George before flowing into Muddy Brook a short distance west of South Brownell Road. This photograph was taken on Lincoln C. Brownell's 11th birthday on June 6, 1925. From left to right are Henry Cornwall, Chauncey Wells Brownell III, Robert Whitney Jr., and Priscilla Brownell enjoying the water of the brook. In 1867, Burlington needed a water supply for the city so a proposal was made to create one or more reservoirs in Sucker Hollow. Thankfully soon after, Burlington turned to Lake Champlain for its water. (Courtesy Bartlett Brownell.)

This 1927 photograph shows Chauncey W. Brownell II (left) and Henry O. Whitney on the concrete dam across Sucker Brook. This was an improvement on a c. 1919 dam built to create a pond near the weekend cabin seen in the background. The pond was a favorite place for children and adults to play on the Brownell homestead. Whitney was the son of William F. Whitney and Zeruah (Brownell) Whitney and an Essex Junction businessman. (Courtesy Bartlett Brownell.)

This was the crude bridge over Sucker Brook south of the Brownell homestead in 1916. The town called on residents to help with the maintenance of roads and bridges and recorded their names and payments in the town reports. They were typically farmers who lived nearby and had the machinery, horse teams, tools, and know-how to tackle such a job. (Courtesy Bartlett Brownell.)

Allen Brook flows out of Mud Pond, heads north through the village, and then west and north to empty into Muddy Brook just before the Winooski River. Emerson Miles Jr. remembers how it provided hours of entertainment for children, with a place to fish, catch frogs, swim, and skate in the winter. The landscape was much different because the cows kept the grass trimmed and it was "like a lawn," not the overgrown "mess" it has become. The spring thaw caused the brook to overflow the North Williston Road bridge. This photograph shows the brook passing under Route 2 at the concrete pedestrian bridge. (Courtesy WHS.)

The southwest corner of Williston is depicted in this detail from the 1857 Walling map of Chittenden County. Ferris Hill, probably a reference to the Ferris family of neighboring St. George, dominates the scene and Shelburne Pond appears at lower left. The 1906 topographical map has the prominence labeled as Brownell Mountain. In the early 1900s, the mountain became a popular hiking destination for Scout and school groups. (Author's collection.)

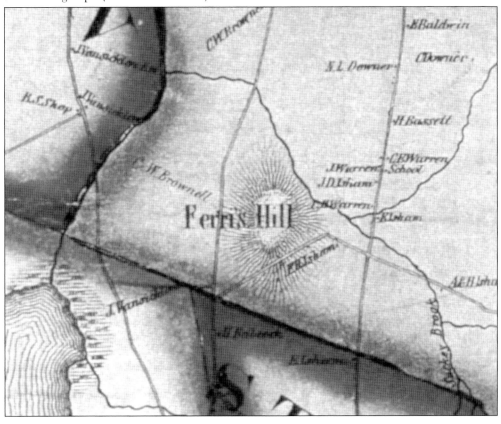

mels Hump near French Hill.

This early-1900s postcard shows the dirt road on French Hill. For motorists traveling between Burlington and Montpelier, this was one of the most dreaded stretches. As early as 1917, plans were drawn up to improve the road by straightening some of the curves and reducing the grade. Numerous accidents and the frustration of negotiating the approximate 235-foot climb in the winter made headlines constantly. In the 1930s, dozens of cars could be stuck at the bottom of the hill for up to two hours waiting for a sand truck to deal with the snow and ice. It was so notorious that one car dealer used it to promote sales. In 1916, E.A. Brodie of Burlington named several local hills that challenged drivers, including Colchester's Sunderland Hollow "and in Williston the still worse French Hill." But the power of the Hupmobile made "all these hills . . . easy meat." Emerson Miles Jr. had a paper route in the 1940s that he finished before school. One day, the roads were all covered with ice, so he put his skates on and "did the route in record time." (Courtesy WHS.)

The route of the Winooski Turnpike became part of the Theodore Roosevelt International Highway shortly after his death in 1919. This ran from Portland, Maine, to Portland, Oregon, and was part of the "auto trail" network of marked routes to encourage exploration by motorists. In 1926, it officially became Route 2, and in 1927, it was paved through the village. A December 1928 advertisement for a 50¢ chicken pie supper at the Federated Church included the reassurance for nervous winter drivers that the "pavement [was] completed to Williston Village." Here, the "hard top" Route 2 on French Hill passes Twist O'Hill Lodge. (Courtesy WHS.)

Photographer Wilbur C. Sawyer captured this train crossing the Winooski River on the trestle between Williston and Essex around 1900. The wooden supports did not meet the challenge of adding heavier and faster rail stock to an existing infrastructure in need of upgrading. Wooden trestles were susceptible to fire, such as the 1855 conflagration that destroyed the Clark bridge that connected Richmond and Williston. (Courtesy Vermont Historical Society.)

The 1927 flood did a great deal of damage to the Vermont railroads, resulting in repaired and replaced trestles built to withstand future tests. This September 22, 1928, photograph shows the deck plate girder replacement trestle, with additional concrete abutments, across the Winooski River just east of the present Global Foundries plant in Essex. (Courtesy WHS.)

The 1927 flood also caused extensive damage to the roads and farms in North Williston. This photograph taken on November 4 looks north across the Winooski Valley to Essex. The Chapman farm (center, behind trees) is surrounded by water. Marvin "Bob" Chapman, then nine, recalled the sound of apples floating in the basement and hitting the ceiling. The cows were led out, and the families soon followed by wading through the water to the railroad tracks. The houses and barns floating downstream were a horrifying sight. (Courtesy WHS.)

The view from Essex across the raging Winooski River to Williston shows the water topping the dam and the bridge on November 4, 1927. Both structures held against the onslaught. Other areas of Williston were also heavily impacted. On the Keith farm at the foot of French Hill, the flood was devastating. Thirty-two head of cattle and four horses were lost. The residents of the Union Poor Farm were rescued, but the water reached the top of the house. The barn, full of hay and straw, headed downstream and was set on fire to keep it from damaging the Lime Kiln bridge. (Courtesy WHS.)

This 1962 photograph of Williston starkly illustrates the mark of the Interstate 89 highway construction. The village and the Oak Hill Road bridge are left of center, and the curve and grade on French Hill are to the right. Like the 1849 arrival of the railroad, the interstate brought on increased accessibility and marked commercial growth. Since 1963, when the Richmond to South Burlington interstate section opened, growth has occurred at Taft Corners and the surrounding area. The highway has also helped cement Williston's role as a suburb in the middle of Chittenden County. (Courtesy State of Vermont.)

The 1962 construction of Interstate 89 created grief and anxiety for the Boyer family. Their 205-acre farm, seen in the distance on South Brownell Road, was split into two, and they received inadequate compensation for the land taken. They had settled there 20 years before and loved the location; the extended family made their homes on the property. The county extension service specialist said their plight "was probably one of the worst in the county." The construction proceeded, and today, Boyer Circle with its industrial and commercial development remains as a reminder of the family and farm. (Courtesy Willy LaCasse.)

This 1965 photograph of Taft Corners shows Route 2 headed west toward South Burlington; Route 2A south is off to the left, and north is to the right. At one time, Route 2A south from here was Route 116A. Gas stations dominated the scene with the still-standing Blair farmhouse on the left. The opening of Interstate 89 in November 1963 and the direct access south of Taft Corners made the area a logical target for development. (Courtesy Vermont State Archives and Records Administration.)

This 1981 image of Taft Corners looking north shows a minimum amount of development and the predominance of farmland still in use. The change in this area of town was highly contentious, with the Citizens for Responsible Growth playing a major role in the debate and decision-making process. Forces for and against Pyramid Mall, Walmart, and Maple Tree Place fought it out over the years. Box stores now prevail in the area and add to the town's income with the local option sales tax adopted in 2003 as well as adding to the demand for town services. The debate continues today with the town seeking input on how to create "a vibrant, mixed use downtown area with a strong pedestrian orientation." (Author's collection.)

On July 7, 1984, the Amtrak Montrealer wrecked in an isolated spot off Redmond Road. Rain and water from breached beaver dams undermined the tracks. Traveling at 59 miles per hour, two engines and the baggage car made it across the gap, but the following cars did not. Five people died and about 150 were injured. The accident triggered a widely praised response from 300 rescue workers. An investigation later revealed the radio communication on the train was not working properly, and the dispatcher did not know that the weather service had issued a flash flood warning. (Courtesy Williston Fire Department.)

This was South Brownell Road in 1915, nothing more than a dirt track, typical of the roads in town at the dawning of the automobile age. It was challenging to deal with the elements, and travel by horse-drawn vehicles was slow by modern standards but adequate. As the number of cars and trucks rose and speed increased, there was a demand for wider and eventually hard-top roads. It was often couched in economic terms to accommodate tourists and improve the efficiency of shipping products. (Courtesy Bartlett Brownell.)

Warming temperatures in the spring in Vermont could mean the challenges of mud season. Ralph H. Orth explained the "thawing of the upper few inches of the ground traps layers of water, which liquefy the soil and make travel on dirt roads difficult." Spring vacation for schools could be three weeks, local travel was hindered, and tourists were warned to inquire about road conditions and carry tire chains. Scenes like this team of horses pulling out a mired truck on South Brownell Road in April 1933 were a common sight. (Courtesy Bartlett Brownell.)

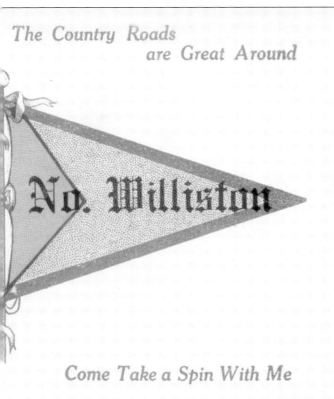

The Country Roads
are Great Around

No. Williston

Come Take a Spin With Me

Even though this generic postcard put a humorous spin on spring thaw, it could be threatening to the local economy. April 1932 was particularly challenging on North Williston Road. With 40,000 to 50,000 pounds of milk trucked each day to the railroad, the road became nearly impassable. After "pleasure cars" got stuck, some locals, "George F. Irish, Charles Miles, Lewis Miles, and Mr. Stone, brushed" the road and filled in on top with nine loads of sand. For these people, this road "was considered the most important highway" in town. The paved Route 2 was fine for those just passing through, opined the *Burlington Free Press*. At times, the mud was so deep that only horses or tractors with chains could get through. People would park their cars near the Federated Church or at the Warren Store and take a tractor, horse-drawn wagon, or walk home. Even in 1955, "the muddy back roads" were bad enough to shut the schools in town. Tommy and Susan Willard, along with Sarah Whitcher and Tommy Bailey, were pictured in the *Burlington Free Press* dealing with stuck bicycles on a muddy road in North Williston. (Courtesy WHS.)

Snowy roads were also a challenge. One early method of dealing with winter's wrath was to pack the snow with horse-drawn rollers, allowing for easier passage by sleighs. Snow was also drawn into the covered bridges for smoother sleighing. With the advent of automobiles, the demand for plowed and sanded roads increased. The 1913 town report lists payment for "winter work" to 22 men. January 1931 brought snow drifts that blocked highways for days, so special rail service was instituted in northern Vermont. This photograph of "Main Street" in North Williston shows what the winter traveler would have to deal with. (Courtesy WHS.)

Burlington bought 50 acres in Williston in 1933. It was a source of sand, gravel, and loam for street construction in the city. Later, trees were planted to create a municipal forest that hopefully would turn a profit when harvested. In 1967, the Greater Burlington Industrial Corporation purchased 46 acres of the land from Burlington to create an industrial park that soon included the Rossignol Ski Company and Johnson Filaments. Rossignol Park is located on a portion of this land along Industrial Avenue. This Louis L. McAllister photograph shows the sandpit in the 1930s. (Courtesy Special Collections, UVM.)

This 1987 view of Sharon Drive, Gail Terrace, and Hillside Drive of Oneida Acres represents the housing developments and population growth off Route 2A. In the 1960s, Meadowbrook boasted of "GE Colorama kitchens, fireplaces, pure spring water, delightful country living near a rushing brook," and Williston Hills had "panelized home[s]" completed in four to five weeks. Lamplite Acres was "3 miles from IBM, paved streets, half-acre treed lots, no pre-fabs, underground wires, rustic streetlights, and homes set back 70 feet," and Oneida Acres lots had "blacktop curbs, roads, storm sewers, water." (Author's collection.)

This covered bridge at Hubbel's Falls served as a connection between Essex and Williston from 1848 to 1927. Previous bridge construction here was contentious and drawn out, and one crossing was wiped out in the 1830 freshet. A sign affixed to the inside of this bridge noted the boundary between the two towns. It was saved by Adolph Lane, the contractor who built the steel bridge that replaced this covered bridge. His son Gordon Lane and daughter Betty (Lane) Bradish donated the sign to the Williston Historical Society. (Courtesy Essex Community Historical Society.)

BIBLIOGRAPHY

Allen, Richard H. *The History of Williston Central School: 1950 to 2000*. Milton, VT: Villanti Printers, 2001.

———. *North Williston: Down Depot Hill*. Charleston, SC: The History Press, 2011.

———. *Ambition and Grit: The Life of Truman Naramore, Civil War Veteran and Entrepreneur*. Burlington, VT: Chittenden County Historical Society, 2015.

———. *Reed Brown's 1841 Journey: America Through the Eyes of a Vermont Yankee*. Burlington, VT: Onion River Press, 2018.

Brownell, Mary Tracy. *Mellow Memories*. Essex Junction, VT: Friends of the Brownell Library, 1999.

Carlisle, Lilian Baker, ed. *Look Around Essex and Williston, Vermont*. Burlington, VT: The Chittenden County Historical Society, 1973.

Dean, Carol B. *The History of Schools in Williston, Vermont*. Privately printed, 1992.

Miles, Emerson J. Jr. "Memoirs of a Boy to Man, Life Style and Home Events." 1992.

Moody, F. Kennon, and Floyd D. Putnam. *The Williston Story*. Essex Junction, VT: The Roscoe Printing House, 1961.

Painter, Ruth. "A Brief Look at Williston, Vermont in the '20s." 1984.

Randall, Willard Sterne, and Nancy Nahra. *Thomas Chittenden's Town: A Story of Williston, Vermont*. Williston, VT: Williston Historical Society, 1998.

Smallwood, Frank. *Thomas Chittenden: Vermont's First Statesman*. Shelburne, VT: The New England Press Inc., 1997.

Wheeler, Dr. John B. *Memoirs of a Small-Town Surgeon*. New York, NY: Frederick A. Stokes Company, 1935.

Williston Revisited: A Community Portrait. Directed by James R. Heltz. Williston, VT: Green Mountain Video Inc., 2013.

Wright, Odella Fay, Sylvia Warren, John Forbes, and Seth Johnson. *A History of the Town of Williston, 1763–1913*. Williston, VT: The Historical Committee: 1913, reprinted 1991.

ABOUT THE WILLISTON HISTORICAL SOCIETY

The Williston Historical Society was established in 1974 to preserve and present the history of Williston. Over the years, we have sponsored publications, lectures, and activities that brought our history to the forefront. The town's Fourth of July celebrations, the 1976 national bicentennial, and the 1991 state bicentennial have all served to focus many of these efforts. The Vermont Room in the Dorothy Alling Memorial Library holds the artifacts and collections of the society, and our newsletter is published in the spring and the fall. Membership is open to all who share an interest in Williston's history, and we always welcome new members and volunteers. Please consider donating your photographs and other material on Williston or letting us scan them to add to our collections for future projects. We are interested in all facets of the town's history: businesses, recreation, celebrations, family life, and everyday activities. Besides photographs, we also collect ephemera such as business cards, advertisements, and announcements. (The Williston Historical Society logo, seen below, was created by Nancy Stone.)

Williston Historical Society
PO Box 995
Williston, Vermont 05495
willistonhistoricalsociety@gmail.com / willistonvtcollections@gmail.com (archivist)
www.willistonhistoricalsociety.org
www.facebook.com/willistonhistoricalsociety

Discover Thousands of Local History Books
Featuring Millions of Vintage Images

Arcadia Publishing, the leading local history publisher in the United States, is committed to making history accessible and meaningful through publishing books that celebrate and preserve the heritage of America's people and places.

Find more books like this at
www.arcadiapublishing.com

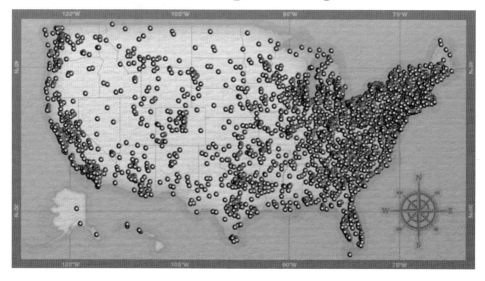

Search for your hometown history, your old stomping grounds, and even your favorite sports team.

Consistent with our mission to preserve history on a local level, this book was printed in South Carolina on American-made paper and manufactured entirely in the United States. Products carrying the accredited Forest Stewardship Council (FSC) label are printed on 100 percent FSC-certified paper.